CS-15  GENERAL APTITUDE AND ABILITIES SERIES

*This is your*
*PASSBOOK for...*

# Mechanical Aptitude

*Test Preparation Study Guide*
*Questions & Answers*

# COPYRIGHT NOTICE

This book is SOLELY intended for, is sold ONLY to, and its use is RESTRICTED to individual, bona fide applicants or candidates who qualify by virtue of having seriously filed applications for appropriate license, certificate, professional and/or promotional advancement, higher school matriculation, scholarship, or other legitimate requirements of education and/or governmental authorities.

This book is NOT intended for use, class instruction, tutoring, training, duplication, copying, reprinting, excerption, or adaptation, etc., by:

1) Other publishers
2) Proprietors and/or Instructors of "Coaching" and/or Preparatory Courses
3) Personnel and/or Training Divisions of commercial, industrial, and governmental organizations
4) Schools, colleges, or universities and/or their departments and staffs, including teachers and other personnel
5) Testing Agencies or Bureaus
6) Study groups which seek by the purchase of a single volume to copy and/or duplicate and/or adapt this material for use by the group as a whole without having purchased individual volumes for each of the members of the group
7) Et al.

Such persons would be in violation of appropriate Federal and State statutes.

PROVISION OF LICENSING AGREEMENTS – Recognized educational, commercial, industrial, and governmental institutions and organizations, and others legitimately engaged in educational pursuits, including training, testing, and measurement activities, may address request for a licensing agreement to the copyright owners, who will determine whether, and under what conditions, including fees and charges, the materials in this book may be used them. In other words, a licensing facility exists for the legitimate use of the material in this book on other than an individual basis. However, it is asseverated and affirmed here that the material in this book CANNOT be used without the receipt of the express permission of such a licensing agreement from the Publishers. Inquiries re licensing should be addressed to the company, attention rights and permissions department.

All rights reserved, including the right of reproduction in whole or in part, in any form or by any means, electronic or mechanical, including photocopying, recording, or by any information storage and retrieval system, without permission in writing from the Publisher.

Copyright © 2024 by
## National Learning Corporation

212 Michael Drive, Syosset, NY 11791
(516) 921-8888 • www.passbooks.com
E-mail: info@passbooks.com

PUBLISHED IN THE UNITED STATES OF AMERICA

# PASSBOOK® SERIES

THE *PASSBOOK® SERIES* has been created to prepare applicants and candidates for the ultimate academic battlefield – the examination room.

At some time in our lives, each and every one of us may be required to take an examination – for validation, matriculation, admission, qualification, registration, certification, or licensure.

Based on the assumption that every applicant or candidate has met the basic formal educational standards, has taken the required number of courses, and read the necessary texts, the *PASSBOOK® SERIES* furnishes the one special preparation which may assure passing with confidence, instead of failing with insecurity. Examination questions – together with answers – are furnished as the basic vehicle for study so that the mysteries of the examination and its compounding difficulties may be eliminated or diminished by a sure method.

This book is meant to help you pass your examination provided that you qualify and are serious in your objective.

The entire field is reviewed through the huge store of content information which is succinctly presented through a provocative and challenging approach – the question-and-answer method.

A climate of success is established by furnishing the correct answers at the end of each test.

You soon learn to recognize types of questions, forms of questions, and patterns of questioning. You may even begin to anticipate expected outcomes.

You perceive that many questions are repeated or adapted so that you can gain acute insights, which may enable you to score many sure points.

You learn how to confront new questions, or types of questions, and to attack them confidently and work out the correct answers.

You note objectives and emphases, and recognize pitfalls and dangers, so that you may make positive educational adjustments.

Moreover, you are kept fully informed in relation to new concepts, methods, practices, and directions in the field.

You discover that you are actually taking the examination all the time: you are preparing for the examination by "taking" an examination, not by reading extraneous and/or supererogatory textbooks.

In short, this PASSBOOK®, used directedly, should be an important factor in helping you to pass your test.

# THE MECHANICAL APTITUDE/COMPREHENSION TEST

The Mechanical Aptitude /Comprehension test evaluates skills indicative of success in a wide range of mechanical related occupations.

The areas covered vary by company or organization, but usually include some or all of the following areas as well as others:

Tools, belt drives, center of gravity, optics, centrifugal force, planes and slopes, electricity, pulley systems, gears, resolution of forces, inertia, gravity and velocity, shape and volume, heat, structures, hydraulics, and miscellaneous others.

# HOW TO TAKE A TEST

I. YOU MUST PASS AN EXAMINATION

A. *WHAT EVERY CANDIDATE SHOULD KNOW*

Examination applicants often ask us for help in preparing for the written test. What can I study in advance? What kinds of questions will be asked? How will the test be given? How will the papers be graded?

As an applicant for a civil service examination, you may be wondering about some of these things. Our purpose here is to suggest effective methods of advance study and to describe civil service examinations.

Your chances for success on this examination can be increased if you know how to prepare. Those "pre-examination jitters" can be reduced if you know what to expect. You can even experience an adventure in good citizenship if you know why civil service exams are given.

B. *WHY ARE CIVIL SERVICE EXAMINATIONS GIVEN?*

Civil service examinations are important to you in two ways. As a citizen, you want public jobs filled by employees who know how to do their work. As a job seeker, you want a fair chance to compete for that job on an equal footing with other candidates. The best-known means of accomplishing this two-fold goal is the competitive examination.

Exams are widely publicized throughout the nation. They may be administered for jobs in federal, state, city, municipal, town or village governments or agencies.

Any citizen may apply, with some limitations, such as the age or residence of applicants. Your experience and education may be reviewed to see whether you meet the requirements for the particular examination. When these requirements exist, they are reasonable and applied consistently to all applicants. Thus, a competitive examination may cause you some uneasiness now, but it is your privilege and safeguard.

C. *HOW ARE CIVIL SERVICE EXAMS DEVELOPED?*

Examinations are carefully written by trained technicians who are specialists in the field known as "psychological measurement," in consultation with recognized authorities in the field of work that the test will cover. These experts recommend the subject matter areas or skills to be tested; only those knowledges or skills important to your success on the job are included. The most reliable books and source materials available are used as references. Together, the experts and technicians judge the difficulty level of the questions.

Test technicians know how to phrase questions so that the problem is clearly stated. Their ethics do not permit "trick" or "catch" questions. Questions may have been tried out on sample groups, or subjected to statistical analysis, to determine their usefulness.

Written tests are often used in combination with performance tests, ratings of training and experience, and oral interviews. All of these measures combine to form the best-known means of finding the right person for the right job.

## II. HOW TO PASS THE WRITTEN TEST

### A. NATURE OF THE EXAMINATION

To prepare intelligently for civil service examinations, you should know how they differ from school examinations you have taken. In school you were assigned certain definite pages to read or subjects to cover. The examination questions were quite detailed and usually emphasized memory. Civil service exams, on the other hand, try to discover your present ability to perform the duties of a position, plus your potentiality to learn these duties. In other words, a civil service exam attempts to predict how successful you will be. Questions cover such a broad area that they cannot be as minute and detailed as school exam questions.

In the public service similar kinds of work, or positions, are grouped together in one "class." This process is known as *position-classification*. All the positions in a class are paid according to the salary range for that class. One class title covers all of these positions, and they are all tested by the same examination.

### B. FOUR BASIC STEPS

#### 1) Study the announcement

How, then, can you know what subjects to study? Our best answer is: "Learn as much as possible about the class of positions for which you've applied." The exam will test the knowledge, skills and abilities needed to do the work.

Your most valuable source of information about the position you want is the official exam announcement. This announcement lists the training and experience qualifications. Check these standards and apply only if you come reasonably close to meeting them.

The brief description of the position in the examination announcement offers some clues to the subjects which will be tested. Think about the job itself. Review the duties in your mind. Can you perform them, or are there some in which you are rusty? Fill in the blank spots in your preparation.

Many jurisdictions preview the written test in the exam announcement by including a section called "Knowledge and Abilities Required," "Scope of the Examination," or some similar heading. Here you will find out specifically what fields will be tested.

#### 2) Review your own background

Once you learn in general what the position is all about, and what you need to know to do the work, ask yourself which subjects you already know fairly well and which need improvement. You may wonder whether to concentrate on improving your strong areas or on building some background in your fields of weakness. When the announcement has specified "some knowledge" or "considerable knowledge," or has used adjectives like "beginning principles of..." or "advanced ... methods," you can get a clue as to the number and difficulty of questions to be asked in any given field. More questions, and hence broader coverage, would be included for those subjects which are more important in the work. Now weigh your strengths and weaknesses against the job requirements and prepare accordingly.

#### 3) Determine the level of the position

Another way to tell how intensively you should prepare is to understand the level of the job for which you are applying. Is it the entering level? In other words, is this the position in which beginners in a field of work are hired? Or is it an intermediate or advanced level? Sometimes this is indicated by such words as "Junior" or "Senior" in the class title. Other jurisdictions use Roman numerals to designate the level – Clerk I, Clerk II, for example. The word "Supervisor" sometimes appears in the title. If the level is not indicated by the title, check the description of duties. Will you be working under very close supervision, or will you have responsibility for independent decisions in this work?

**4) Choose appropriate study materials**

Now that you know the subjects to be examined and the relative amount of each subject to be covered, you can choose suitable study materials. For beginning level jobs, or even advanced ones, if you have a pronounced weakness in some aspect of your training, read a modern, standard textbook in that field. Be sure it is up to date and has general coverage. Such books are normally available at your library, and the librarian will be glad to help you locate one. For entry-level positions, questions of appropriate difficulty are chosen – neither highly advanced questions, nor those too simple. Such questions require careful thought but not advanced training.

If the position for which you are applying is technical or advanced, you will read more advanced, specialized material. If you are already familiar with the basic principles of your field, elementary textbooks would waste your time. Concentrate on advanced textbooks and technical periodicals. Think through the concepts and review difficult problems in your field.

These are all general sources. You can get more ideas on your own initiative, following these leads. For example, training manuals and publications of the government agency which employs workers in your field can be useful, particularly for technical and professional positions. A letter or visit to the government department involved may result in more specific study suggestions, and certainly will provide you with a more definite idea of the exact nature of the position you are seeking.

## III. KINDS OF TESTS

Tests are used for purposes other than measuring knowledge and ability to perform specified duties. For some positions, it is equally important to test ability to make adjustments to new situations or to profit from training. In others, basic mental abilities not dependent on information are essential. Questions which test these things may not appear as pertinent to the duties of the position as those which test for knowledge and information. Yet they are often highly important parts of a fair examination. For very general questions, it is almost impossible to help you direct your study efforts. What we can do is to point out some of the more common of these general abilities needed in public service positions and describe some typical questions.

1) General information

Broad, general information has been found useful for predicting job success in some kinds of work. This is tested in a variety of ways, from vocabulary lists to questions about current events. Basic background in some field of work, such as sociology or economics, may be sampled in a group of questions. Often these are principles which have become familiar to most persons through exposure rather than through formal training. It is difficult to advise you how to study for these questions; being alert to the world around you is our best suggestion.

2) Verbal ability

An example of an ability needed in many positions is verbal or language ability. Verbal ability is, in brief, the ability to use and understand words. Vocabulary and grammar tests are typical measures of this ability. Reading comprehension or paragraph interpretation questions are common in many kinds of civil service tests. You are given a paragraph of written material and asked to find its central meaning.

3) Numerical ability

Number skills can be tested by the familiar arithmetic problem, by checking paired lists of numbers to see which are alike and which are different, or by interpreting charts and graphs. In the latter test, a graph may be printed in the test booklet which you are asked to use as the basis for answering questions.

4) Observation

A popular test for law-enforcement positions is the observation test. A picture is shown to you for several minutes, then taken away. Questions about the picture test your ability to observe both details and larger elements.

5) Following directions

In many positions in the public service, the employee must be able to carry out written instructions dependably and accurately. You may be given a chart with several columns, each column listing a variety of information. The questions require you to carry out directions involving the information given in the chart.

6) Skills and aptitudes

Performance tests effectively measure some manual skills and aptitudes. When the skill is one in which you are trained, such as typing or shorthand, you can practice. These tests are often very much like those given in business school or high school courses. For many of the other skills and aptitudes, however, no short-time preparation can be made. Skills and abilities natural to you or that you have developed throughout your lifetime are being tested.

Many of the general questions just described provide all the data needed to answer the questions and ask you to use your reasoning ability to find the answers. Your best preparation for these tests, as well as for tests of facts and ideas, is to be at your physical and mental best. You, no doubt, have your own methods of getting into an exam-taking mood and keeping "in shape." The next section lists some ideas on this subject.


IV. KINDS OF QUESTIONS

Only rarely is the "essay" question, which you answer in narrative form, used in civil service tests. Civil service tests are usually of the short-answer type. Full instructions for answering these questions will be given to you at the examination. But in case this is your first experience with short-answer questions and separate answer sheets, here is what you need to know:

**1) Multiple-choice Questions**

Most popular of the short-answer questions is the "multiple choice" or "best answer" question. It can be used, for example, to test for factual knowledge, ability to solve problems or judgment in meeting situations found at work.

A multiple-choice question is normally one of three types—
- It can begin with an incomplete statement followed by several possible endings. You are to find the one ending which *best* completes the statement, although some of the others may not be entirely wrong.
- It can also be a complete statement in the form of a question which is answered by choosing one of the statements listed.

- It can be in the form of a problem – again you select the best answer.

Here is an example of a multiple-choice question with a discussion which should give you some clues as to the method for choosing the right answer:

When an employee has a complaint about his assignment, the action which will *best* help him overcome his difficulty is to
- A. discuss his difficulty with his coworkers
- B. take the problem to the head of the organization
- C. take the problem to the person who gave him the assignment
- D. say nothing to anyone about his complaint

In answering this question, you should study each of the choices to find which is best. Consider choice "A" – Certainly an employee may discuss his complaint with fellow employees, but no change or improvement can result, and the complaint remains unresolved. Choice "B" is a poor choice since the head of the organization probably does not know what assignment you have been given, and taking your problem to him is known as "going over the head" of the supervisor. The supervisor, or person who made the assignment, is the person who can clarify it or correct any injustice. Choice "C" is, therefore, correct. To say nothing, as in choice "D," is unwise. Supervisors have and interest in knowing the problems employees are facing, and the employee is seeking a solution to his problem.

## 2) True/False Questions

The "true/false" or "right/wrong" form of question is sometimes used. Here a complete statement is given. Your job is to decide whether the statement is right or wrong.

SAMPLE: A roaming cell-phone call to a nearby city costs less than a non-roaming call to a distant city.

This statement is wrong, or false, since roaming calls are more expensive.

This is not a complete list of all possible question forms, although most of the others are variations of these common types. You will always get complete directions for answering questions. Be sure you understand *how* to mark your answers – ask questions until you do.

## V. RECORDING YOUR ANSWERS

Computer terminals are used more and more today for many different kinds of exams.

For an examination with very few applicants, you may be told to record your answers in the test booklet itself. Separate answer sheets are much more common. If this separate answer sheet is to be scored by machine – and this is often the case – it is highly important that you mark your answers correctly in order to get credit.

An electronic scoring machine is often used in civil service offices because of the speed with which papers can be scored. Machine-scored answer sheets must be marked with a pencil, which will be given to you. This pencil has a high graphite content which responds to the electronic scoring machine. As a matter of fact, stray dots may register as answers, so do not let your pencil rest on the answer sheet while you are pondering the correct answer. Also, if your pencil lead breaks or is otherwise defective, ask for another.

Since the answer sheet will be dropped in a slot in the scoring machine, be careful not to bend the corners or get the paper crumpled.

The answer sheet normally has five vertical columns of numbers, with 30 numbers to a column. These numbers correspond to the question numbers in your test booklet. After each number, going across the page are four or five pairs of dotted lines. These short dotted lines have small letters or numbers above them. The first two pairs may also have a "T" or "F" above the letters. This indicates that the first two pairs only are to be used if the questions are of the true-false type. If the questions are multiple choice, disregard the "T" and "F" and pay attention only to the small letters or numbers.

Answer your questions in the manner of the sample that follows:

32. The largest city in the United States is
    A. Washington, D.C.
    B. New York City
    C. Chicago
    D. Detroit
    E. San Francisco

1) Choose the answer you think is best. (New York City is the largest, so "B" is correct.)
2) Find the row of dotted lines numbered the same as the question you are answering. (Find row number 32)
3) Find the pair of dotted lines corresponding to the answer. (Find the pair of lines under the mark "B.")
4) Make a solid black mark between the dotted lines.

## VI. BEFORE THE TEST

Common sense will help you find procedures to follow to get ready for an examination. Too many of us, however, overlook these sensible measures. Indeed, nervousness and fatigue have been found to be the most serious reasons why applicants fail to do their best on civil service tests. Here is a list of reminders:

- Begin your preparation early – Don't wait until the last minute to go scurrying around for books and materials or to find out what the position is all about.
- Prepare continuously – An hour a night for a week is better than an all-night cram session. This has been definitely established. What is more, a night a week for a month will return better dividends than crowding your study into a shorter period of time.
- Locate the place of the exam – You have been sent a notice telling you when and where to report for the examination. If the location is in a different town or otherwise unfamiliar to you, it would be well to inquire the best route and learn something about the building.
- Relax the night before the test – Allow your mind to rest. Do not study at all that night. Plan some mild recreation or diversion; then go to bed early and get a good night's sleep.
- Get up early enough to make a leisurely trip to the place for the test – This way unforeseen events, traffic snarls, unfamiliar buildings, etc. will not upset you.
- Dress comfortably – A written test is not a fashion show. You will be known by number and not by name, so wear something comfortable.

- Leave excess paraphernalia at home – Shopping bags and odd bundles will get in your way. You need bring only the items mentioned in the official notice you received; usually everything you need is provided. Do not bring reference books to the exam. They will only confuse those last minutes and be taken away from you when in the test room.
- Arrive somewhat ahead of time – If because of transportation schedules you must get there very early, bring a newspaper or magazine to take your mind off yourself while waiting.
- Locate the examination room – When you have found the proper room, you will be directed to the seat or part of the room where you will sit. Sometimes you are given a sheet of instructions to read while you are waiting. Do not fill out any forms until you are told to do so; just read them and be prepared.
- Relax and prepare to listen to the instructions
- If you have any physical problem that may keep you from doing your best, be sure to tell the test administrator. If you are sick or in poor health, you really cannot do your best on the exam. You can come back and take the test some other time.

## VII. AT THE TEST

The day of the test is here and you have the test booklet in your hand. The temptation to get going is very strong. Caution! There is more to success than knowing the right answers. You must know how to identify your papers and understand variations in the type of short-answer question used in this particular examination. Follow these suggestions for maximum results from your efforts:

### 1) Cooperate with the monitor

The test administrator has a duty to create a situation in which you can be as much at ease as possible. He will give instructions, tell you when to begin, check to see that you are marking your answer sheet correctly, and so on. He is not there to guard you, although he will see that your competitors do not take unfair advantage. He wants to help you do your best.

### 2) Listen to all instructions

Don't jump the gun! Wait until you understand all directions. In most civil service tests you get more time than you need to answer the questions. So don't be in a hurry. Read each word of instructions until you clearly understand the meaning. Study the examples, listen to all announcements and follow directions. Ask questions if you do not understand what to do.

### 3) Identify your papers

Civil service exams are usually identified by number only. You will be assigned a number; you must not put your name on your test papers. Be sure to copy your number correctly. Since more than one exam may be given, copy your exact examination title.

### 4) Plan your time

Unless you are told that a test is a "speed" or "rate of work" test, speed itself is usually not important. Time enough to answer all the questions will be provided, but this does not mean that you have all day. An overall time limit has been set. Divide the total time (in minutes) by the number of questions to determine the approximate time you have for each question.

### 5) Do not linger over difficult questions

If you come across a difficult question, mark it with a paper clip (useful to have along) and come back to it when you have been through the booklet. One caution if you do this – be sure to skip a number on your answer sheet as well. Check often to be sure that you have not lost your place and that you are marking in the row numbered the same as the question you are answering.

### 6) Read the questions

Be sure you know what the question asks! Many capable people are unsuccessful because they failed to *read* the questions correctly.

### 7) Answer all questions

Unless you have been instructed that a penalty will be deducted for incorrect answers, it is better to guess than to omit a question.

### 8) Speed tests

It is often better NOT to guess on speed tests. It has been found that on timed tests people are tempted to spend the last few seconds before time is called in marking answers at random – without even reading them – in the hope of picking up a few extra points. To discourage this practice, the instructions may warn you that your score will be "corrected" for guessing. That is, a penalty will be applied. The incorrect answers will be deducted from the correct ones, or some other penalty formula will be used.

### 9) Review your answers

If you finish before time is called, go back to the questions you guessed or omitted to give them further thought. Review other answers if you have time.

### 10) Return your test materials

If you are ready to leave before others have finished or time is called, take ALL your materials to the monitor and leave quietly. Never take any test material with you. The monitor can discover whose papers are not complete, and taking a test booklet may be grounds for disqualification.

## VIII. EXAMINATION TECHNIQUES

1) Read the general instructions carefully. These are usually printed on the first page of the exam booklet. As a rule, these instructions refer to the timing of the examination; the fact that you should not start work until the signal and must stop work at a signal, etc. If there are any *special* instructions, such as a choice of questions to be answered, make sure that you note this instruction carefully.

2) When you are ready to start work on the examination, that is as soon as the signal has been given, read the instructions to each question booklet, underline any key words or phrases, such as *least, best, outline, describe* and the like. In this way you will tend to answer as requested rather than discover on reviewing your paper that you *listed without describing*, that you selected the *worst* choice rather than the *best* choice, etc.

3) If the examination is of the objective or multiple-choice type – that is, each question will also give a series of possible answers: A, B, C or D, and you are called upon to select the best answer and write the letter next to that answer on your answer paper – it is advisable to start answering each question in turn. There may be anywhere from 50 to 100 such questions in the three or four hours allotted and you can see how much time would be taken if you read through all the questions before beginning to answer any. Furthermore, if you come across a question or group of questions which you know would be difficult to answer, it would undoubtedly affect your handling of all the other questions.

4) If the examination is of the essay type and contains but a few questions, it is a moot point as to whether you should read all the questions before starting to answer any one. Of course, if you are given a choice – say five out of seven and the like – then it is essential to read all the questions so you can eliminate the two that are most difficult. If, however, you are asked to answer all the questions, there may be danger in trying to answer the easiest one first because you may find that you will spend too much time on it. The best technique is to answer the first question, then proceed to the second, etc.

5) Time your answers. Before the exam begins, write down the time it started, then add the time allowed for the examination and write down the time it must be completed, then divide the time available somewhat as follows:
    - If 3-1/2 hours are allowed, that would be 210 minutes. If you have 80 objective-type questions, that would be an average of 2-1/2 minutes per question. Allow yourself no more than 2 minutes per question, or a total of 160 minutes, which will permit about 50 minutes to review.
    - If for the time allotment of 210 minutes there are 7 essay questions to answer, that would average about 30 minutes a question. Give yourself only 25 minutes per question so that you have about 35 minutes to review.

6) The most important instruction is to *read each question* and make sure you know what is wanted. The second most important instruction is to *time yourself properly* so that you answer every question. The third most important instruction is to *answer every question*. Guess if you have to but include something for each question. Remember that you will receive no credit for a blank and will probably receive some credit if you write something in answer to an essay question. If you guess a letter – say "B" for a multiple-choice question – you may have guessed right. If you leave a blank as an answer to a multiple-choice question, the examiners may respect your feelings but it will not add a point to your score. Some exams may penalize you for wrong answers, so in such cases *only*, you may not want to guess unless you have some basis for your answer.

7) Suggestions
    a. Objective-type questions
        1. Examine the question booklet for proper sequence of pages and questions
        2. Read all instructions carefully
        3. Skip any question which seems too difficult; return to it after all other questions have been answered
        4. Apportion your time properly; do not spend too much time on any single question or group of questions

5. Note and underline key words – *all, most, fewest, least, best, worst, same, opposite*, etc.
6. Pay particular attention to negatives
7. Note unusual option, e.g., unduly long, short, complex, different or similar in content to the body of the question
8. Observe the use of "hedging" words – *probably, may, most likely*, etc.
9. Make sure that your answer is put next to the same number as the question
10. Do not second-guess unless you have good reason to believe the second answer is definitely more correct
11. Cross out original answer if you decide another answer is more accurate; do not erase until you are ready to hand your paper in
12. Answer all questions; guess unless instructed otherwise
13. Leave time for review

b. Essay questions
1. Read each question carefully
2. Determine exactly what is wanted. Underline key words or phrases.
3. Decide on outline or paragraph answer
4. Include many different points and elements unless asked to develop any one or two points or elements
5. Show impartiality by giving pros and cons unless directed to select one side only
6. Make and write down any assumptions you find necessary to answer the questions
7. Watch your English, grammar, punctuation and choice of words
8. Time your answers; don't crowd material

8) Answering the essay question

Most essay questions can be answered by framing the specific response around several key words or ideas. Here are a few such key words or ideas:

M's: manpower, materials, methods, money, management
P's: purpose, program, policy, plan, procedure, practice, problems, pitfalls, personnel, public relations

a. Six basic steps in handling problems:
1. Preliminary plan and background development
2. Collect information, data and facts
3. Analyze and interpret information, data and facts
4. Analyze and develop solutions as well as make recommendations
5. Prepare report and sell recommendations
6. Install recommendations and follow up effectiveness

b. Pitfalls to avoid
1. *Taking things for granted* – A statement of the situation does not necessarily imply that each of the elements is necessarily true; for example, a complaint may be invalid and biased so that all that can be taken for granted is that a complaint has been registered

2. *Considering only one side of a situation* – Wherever possible, indicate several alternatives and then point out the reasons you selected the best one
3. *Failing to indicate follow up* – Whenever your answer indicates action on your part, make certain that you will take proper follow-up action to see how successful your recommendations, procedures or actions turn out to be
4. *Taking too long in answering any single question* – Remember to time your answers properly

## IX. AFTER THE TEST

Scoring procedures differ in detail among civil service jurisdictions although the general principles are the same. Whether the papers are hand-scored or graded by machine we have described, they are nearly always graded by number. That is, the person who marks the paper knows only the number – never the name – of the applicant. Not until all the papers have been graded will they be matched with names. If other tests, such as training and experience or oral interview ratings have been given, scores will be combined. Different parts of the examination usually have different weights. For example, the written test might count 60 percent of the final grade, and a rating of training and experience 40 percent. In many jurisdictions, veterans will have a certain number of points added to their grades.

After the final grade has been determined, the names are placed in grade order and an eligible list is established. There are various methods for resolving ties between those who get the same final grade – probably the most common is to place first the name of the person whose application was received first. Job offers are made from the eligible list in the order the names appear on it. You will be notified of your grade and your rank as soon as all these computations have been made. This will be done as rapidly as possible.

People who are found to meet the requirements in the announcement are called "eligibles." Their names are put on a list of eligible candidates. An eligible's chances of getting a job depend on how high he stands on this list and how fast agencies are filling jobs from the list.

When a job is to be filled from a list of eligibles, the agency asks for the names of people on the list of eligibles for that job. When the civil service commission receives this request, it sends to the agency the names of the three people highest on this list. Or, if the job to be filled has specialized requirements, the office sends the agency the names of the top three persons who meet these requirements from the general list.

The appointing officer makes a choice from among the three people whose names were sent to him. If the selected person accepts the appointment, the names of the others are put back on the list to be considered for future openings.

That is the rule in hiring from all kinds of eligible lists, whether they are for typist, carpenter, chemist, or something else. For every vacancy, the appointing officer has his choice of any one of the top three eligibles on the list. This explains why the person whose name is on top of the list sometimes does not get an appointment when some of the persons lower on the list do. If the appointing officer chooses the second or third eligible, the No. 1 eligible does not get a job at once, but stays on the list until he is appointed or the list is terminated.

# X. HOW TO PASS THE INTERVIEW TEST

The examination for which you applied requires an oral interview test. You have already taken the written test and you are now being called for the interview test – the final part of the formal examination.

You may think that it is not possible to prepare for an interview test and that there are no procedures to follow during an interview. Our purpose is to point out some things you can do in advance that will help you and some good rules to follow and pitfalls to avoid while you are being interviewed.

*What is an interview supposed to test?*

The written examination is designed to test the technical knowledge and competence of the candidate; the oral is designed to evaluate intangible qualities, not readily measured otherwise, and to establish a list showing the relative fitness of each candidate – as measured against his competitors – for the position sought. Scoring is not on the basis of "right" and "wrong," but on a sliding scale of values ranging from "not passable" to "outstanding." As a matter of fact, it is possible to achieve a relatively low score without a single "incorrect" answer because of evident weakness in the qualities being measured.

Occasionally, an examination may consist entirely of an oral test – either an individual or a group oral. In such cases, information is sought concerning the technical knowledges and abilities of the candidate, since there has been no written examination for this purpose. More commonly, however, an oral test is used to supplement a written examination.

*Who conducts interviews?*

The composition of oral boards varies among different jurisdictions. In nearly all, a representative of the personnel department serves as chairman. One of the members of the board may be a representative of the department in which the candidate would work. In some cases, "outside experts" are used, and, frequently, a businessman or some other representative of the general public is asked to serve. Labor and management or other special groups may be represented. The aim is to secure the services of experts in the appropriate field.

However the board is composed, it is a good idea (and not at all improper or unethical) to ascertain in advance of the interview who the members are and what groups they represent. When you are introduced to them, you will have some idea of their backgrounds and interests, and at least you will not stutter and stammer over their names.

*What should be done before the interview?*

While knowledge about the board members is useful and takes some of the surprise element out of the interview, there is other preparation which is more substantive. It *is* possible to prepare for an oral interview – in several ways:

### 1) Keep a copy of your application and review it carefully before the interview

This may be the only document before the oral board, and the starting point of the interview. Know what education and experience you have listed there, and the sequence and dates of all of it. Sometimes the board will ask you to review the highlights of your experience for them; you should not have to hem and haw doing it.

### 2) Study the class specification and the examination announcement

Usually, the oral board has one or both of these to guide them. The qualities, characteristics or knowledges required by the position sought are stated in these documents. They offer valuable clues as to the nature of the oral interview. For example, if the job involves supervisory responsibilities, the announcement will usually indicate that knowledge of modern supervisory methods and the qualifications of the candidate as a supervisor will be tested. If so, you can expect such questions, frequently in the form of a hypothetical situation which you are expected to solve. NEVER go into an oral without knowledge of the duties and responsibilities of the job you seek.

### 3) Think through each qualification required

Try to visualize the kind of questions you would ask if you were a board member. How well could you answer them? Try especially to appraise your own knowledge and background in each area, *measured against the job sought*, and identify any areas in which you are weak. Be critical and realistic – do not flatter yourself.

### 4) Do some general reading in areas in which you feel you may be weak

For example, if the job involves supervision and your past experience has NOT, some general reading in supervisory methods and practices, particularly in the field of human relations, might be useful. Do NOT study agency procedures or detailed manuals. The oral board will be testing your understanding and capacity, not your memory.

### 5) Get a good night's sleep and watch your general health and mental attitude

You will want a clear head at the interview. Take care of a cold or any other minor ailment, and of course, no hangovers.

*What should be done on the day of the interview?*

Now comes the day of the interview itself. Give yourself plenty of time to get there. Plan to arrive somewhat ahead of the scheduled time, particularly if your appointment is in the fore part of the day. If a previous candidate fails to appear, the board might be ready for you a bit early. By early afternoon an oral board is almost invariably behind schedule if there are many candidates, and you may have to wait. Take along a book or magazine to read, or your application to review, but leave any extraneous material in the waiting room when you go in for your interview. In any event, relax and compose yourself.

The matter of dress is important. The board is forming impressions about you – from your experience, your manners, your attitude, and your appearance. Give your personal appearance careful attention. Dress your best, but not your flashiest. Choose conservative, appropriate clothing, and be sure it is immaculate. This is a business interview, and your appearance should indicate that you regard it as such. Besides, being well groomed and properly dressed will help boost your confidence.

Sooner or later, someone will call your name and escort you into the interview room. *This is it.* From here on you are on your own. It is too late for any more preparation. But remember, you asked for this opportunity to prove your fitness, and you are here because your request was granted.

*What happens when you go in?*

The usual sequence of events will be as follows: The clerk (who is often the board stenographer) will introduce you to the chairman of the oral board, who will introduce you to the other members of the board. Acknowledge the introductions before you sit down. Do not be surprised if you find a microphone facing you or a stenotypist sitting by. Oral interviews are usually recorded in the event of an appeal or other review.

Usually the chairman of the board will open the interview by reviewing the highlights of your education and work experience from your application – primarily for the benefit of the other members of the board, as well as to get the material into the record. Do not interrupt or comment unless there is an error or significant misinterpretation; if that is the case, do not hesitate. But do not quibble about insignificant matters. Also, he will usually ask you some question about your education, experience or your present job – partly to get you to start talking and to establish the interviewing "rapport." He may start the actual questioning, or turn it over to one of the other members. Frequently, each member undertakes the questioning on a particular area, one in which he is perhaps most competent, so you can expect each member to participate in the examination. Because time is limited, you may also expect some rather abrupt switches in the direction the questioning takes, so do not be upset by it. Normally, a board member will not pursue a single line of questioning unless he discovers a particular strength or weakness.

After each member has participated, the chairman will usually ask whether any member has any further questions, then will ask you if you have anything you wish to add. Unless you are expecting this question, it may floor you. Worse, it may start you off on an extended, extemporaneous speech. The board is not usually seeking more information. The question is principally to offer you a last opportunity to present further qualifications or to indicate that you have nothing to add. So, if you feel that a significant qualification or characteristic has been overlooked, it is proper to point it out in a sentence or so. Do not compliment the board on the thoroughness of their examination – they have been sketchy, and you know it. If you wish, merely say, "No thank you, I have nothing further to add." This is a point where you can "talk yourself out" of a good impression or fail to present an important bit of information. Remember, *you close the interview yourself*.

The chairman will then say, "That is all, Mr. _____, thank you." Do not be startled; the interview is over, and quicker than you think. Thank him, gather your belongings and take your leave. Save your sigh of relief for the other side of the door.


*How to put your best foot forward*

Throughout this entire process, you may feel that the board individually and collectively is trying to pierce your defenses, seek out your hidden weaknesses and embarrass and confuse you. Actually, this is not true. They are obliged to make an appraisal of your qualifications for the job you are seeking, and they want to see you in your best light. Remember, they must interview all candidates and a non-cooperative candidate may become a failure in spite of their best efforts to bring out his qualifications. Here are 15 suggestions that will help you:

**1) Be natural – Keep your attitude confident, not cocky**

If you are not confident that you can do the job, do not expect the board to be. Do not apologize for your weaknesses, try to bring out your strong points. The board is interested in a positive, not negative, presentation. Cockiness will antagonize any board member and make him wonder if you are covering up a weakness by a false show of strength.

**2) Get comfortable, but don't lounge or sprawl**

Sit erectly but not stiffly. A careless posture may lead the board to conclude that you are careless in other things, or at least that you are not impressed by the importance of the occasion. Either conclusion is natural, even if incorrect. Do not fuss with your clothing, a pencil or an ashtray. Your hands may occasionally be useful to emphasize a point; do not let them become a point of distraction.

**3) Do not wisecrack or make small talk**

This is a serious situation, and your attitude should show that you consider it as such. Further, the time of the board is limited – they do not want to waste it, and neither should you.

### 4) Do not exaggerate your experience or abilities

In the first place, from information in the application or other interviews and sources, the board may know more about you than you think. Secondly, you probably will not get away with it. An experienced board is rather adept at spotting such a situation, so do not take the chance.

### 5) If you know a board member, do not make a point of it, yet do not hide it

Certainly you are not fooling him, and probably not the other members of the board. Do not try to take advantage of your acquaintanceship – it will probably do you little good.

### 6) Do not dominate the interview

Let the board do that. They will give you the clues – do not assume that you have to do all the talking. Realize that the board has a number of questions to ask you, and do not try to take up all the interview time by showing off your extensive knowledge of the answer to the first one.

### 7) Be attentive

You only have 20 minutes or so, and you should keep your attention at its sharpest throughout. When a member is addressing a problem or question to you, give him your undivided attention. Address your reply principally to him, but do not exclude the other board members.

### 8) Do not interrupt

A board member may be stating a problem for you to analyze. He will ask you a question when the time comes. Let him state the problem, and wait for the question.

### 9) Make sure you understand the question

Do not try to answer until you are sure what the question is. If it is not clear, restate it in your own words or ask the board member to clarify it for you. However, do not haggle about minor elements.

### 10) Reply promptly but not hastily

A common entry on oral board rating sheets is "candidate responded readily," or "candidate hesitated in replies." Respond as promptly and quickly as you can, but do not jump to a hasty, ill-considered answer.

### 11) Do not be peremptory in your answers

A brief answer is proper – but do not fire your answer back. That is a losing game from your point of view. The board member can probably ask questions much faster than you can answer them.

### 12) Do not try to create the answer you think the board member wants

He is interested in what kind of mind you have and how it works – not in playing games. Furthermore, he can usually spot this practice and will actually grade you down on it.

### 13) Do not switch sides in your reply merely to agree with a board member

Frequently, a member will take a contrary position merely to draw you out and to see if you are willing and able to defend your point of view. Do not start a debate, yet do not surrender a good position. If a position is worth taking, it is worth defending.

### 14) Do not be afraid to admit an error in judgment if you are shown to be wrong

The board knows that you are forced to reply without any opportunity for careful consideration. Your answer may be demonstrably wrong. If so, admit it and get on with the interview.

### 15) Do not dwell at length on your present job

The opening question may relate to your present assignment. Answer the question but do not go into an extended discussion. You are being examined for a *new* job, not your present one. As a matter of fact, try to phrase ALL your answers in terms of the job for which you are being examined.

*Basis of Rating*

Probably you will forget most of these "do's" and "don'ts" when you walk into the oral interview room. Even remembering them all will not ensure you a passing grade. Perhaps you did not have the qualifications in the first place. But remembering them will help you to put your best foot forward, without treading on the toes of the board members.

Rumor and popular opinion to the contrary notwithstanding, an oral board wants you to make the best appearance possible. They know you are under pressure – but they also want to see how you respond to it as a guide to what your reaction would be under the pressures of the job you seek. They will be influenced by the degree of poise you display, the personal traits you show and the manner in which you respond.

## ABOUT THIS BOOK

This book contains tests divided into Examination Sections. Go through each test, answering every question in the margin. We have also attached a sample answer sheet at the back of the book that can be removed and used. At the end of each test look at the answer key and check your answers. On the ones you got wrong, look at the right answer choice and learn. Do not fill in the answers first. Do not memorize the questions and answers, but understand the answer and principles involved. On your test, the questions will likely be different from the samples. Questions are changed and new ones added. If you understand these past questions you should have success with any changes that arise. Tests may consist of several types of questions. We have additional books on each subject should more study be advisable or necessary for you. Finally, the more you study, the better prepared you will be. This book is intended to be the last thing you study before you walk into the examination room. Prior study of relevant texts is also recommended. NLC publishes some of these in our Fundamental Series. Knowledge and good sense are important factors in passing your exam. Good luck also helps. So now study this Passbook, absorb the material contained within and take that knowledge into the examination. Then do your best to pass that exam.

# EXAMINATION SECTION

# MECHANICAL APTITUDE EXAMINATION SECTION
# TEST 1

## MECHANICAL COMPREHENSION

DIRECTIONS: Questions 1 through 4 test your ability to understand general mechanical devices. Pictures are shown and questions asked about the mechanical devices shown in the picture. Read each question and study the picture. Each question is followed by four choices. For each question, choose the one BEST answer (A, B, C, or D). Then, *PRINT THE LETTER OF THE CORRECT ANSWER IN THE SPACE AT THE RIGHT.*

1.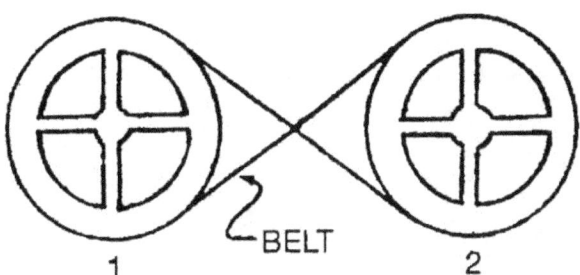

   The reason for crossing the belt connecting these wheels is to
   A. make the wheels turn in opposite directions
   B. make wheel 2 turn faster than wheel 1
   C. save wear on the belt
   D. take up slack in the belt

   1.____

2.

   The purpose of the small gear between the two large gears is to
   A. increase the speed of the larger gears
   B. allow the larger gears to turn in different directions
   C. decrease the speed of the larger gears
   D. make the larger gears turn in the same direction

   2.____

3.

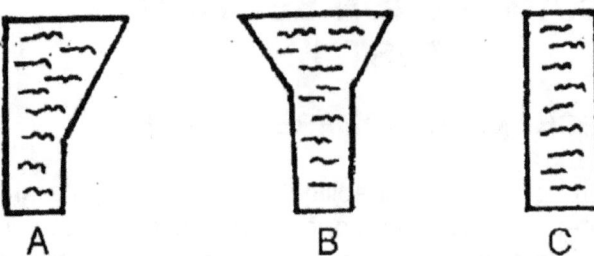

Each of these three-foot-high water cans have a bottom with an area of one square foot.
The pressure on the bottom of the cans is
   A. least in A    B. least in B    C. least in C    D. the same in all

4.

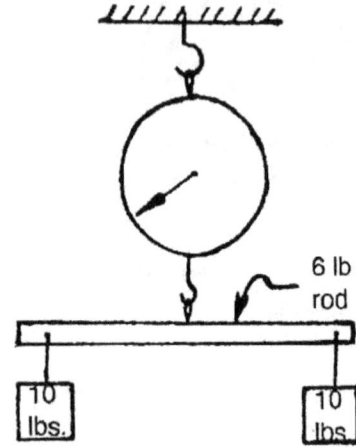

The reading on the scale should be
   A. zero    B. 10 pounds    C. 13 pounds    D. 26 pounds

## KEY (CORRECT ANSWERS)

1. A
2. D
3. D
4. D

# TEST 2

DIRECTIONS: Questions 1 through 6 test knowledge of tools and how to use them. For each question, decide which one of the four things shown in the boxes labeled A, B, C, or D normally is used with or goes best with the thing in the picture on the left. *PRINT THE LETTER OF THE CORRECT ANSWER IN THE SPACE AT THE RIGHT.*

NOTE: All tools are NOT drawn to the same scale.

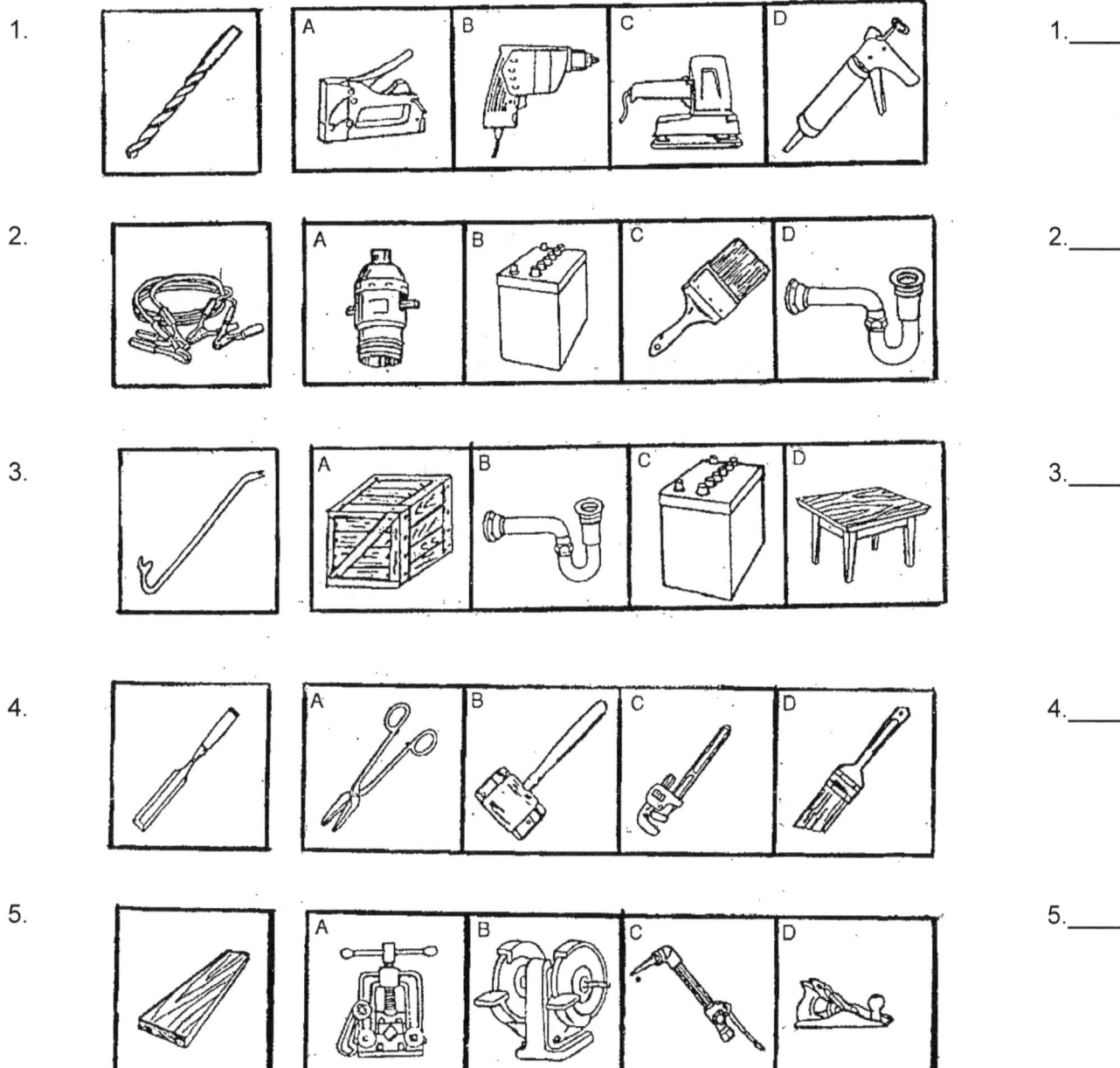

6. 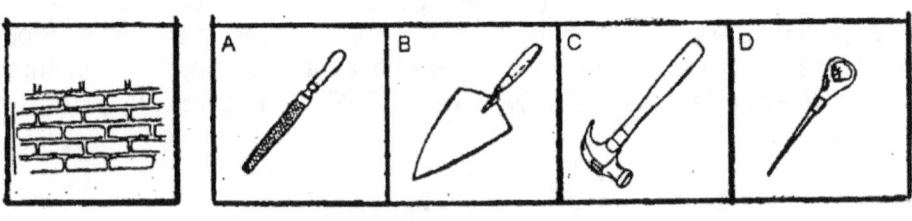  6.____

## KEY (CORRECT ANSWERS)

1. B    4. B
2. B    5. D
3. A    6. B

# MECHANICAL APTITUDE
# EXAMINATION SECTION
## TEST 1

DIRECTIONS: Questions 1 through 6 are questions designed to test your ability to distinguish identical forms from unlike forms. In each question, there are five drawings, lettered A, B, C, D, and E. Four of the drawings are alike. You are to find the one drawing that is different from the other four in the question *PRINT THE LETTER OF THE CORRECT ANSWER IN THE SPACE AT THE RIGHT.*

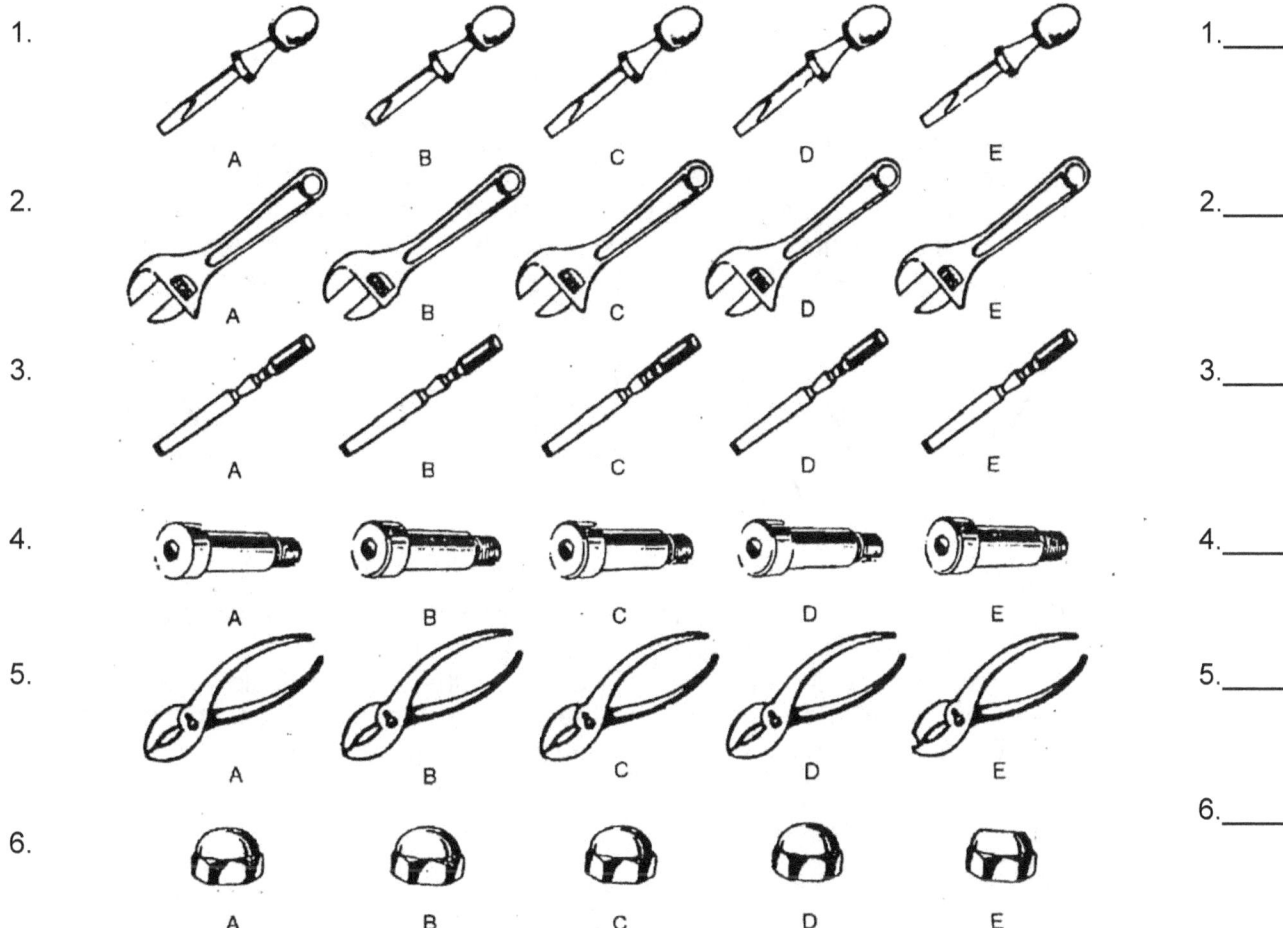

1.\_\_\_\_

2.\_\_\_\_

3.\_\_\_\_

4.\_\_\_\_

5.\_\_\_\_

6.\_\_\_\_

Questions 7-8.

DIRECTIONS: Questions 7 and 8 are questions designed to test your knowledge of pattern matching. Questions 7 and 8 present problems found in making patterns. Each shows, at the left side, two or more separate flat pieces. In each question, select the arrangement lettered A, B, C, or D that shows how these pieces may be turned around or turned over in any way to make them fit together

7.        7.____

   A　　　　B　　　　C　　　　D

From these pieces, which one of these arrangements can you make?

In Question 7, only the arrangement D can be made from the pieces shown at the left, so space choice D should be printed in the space at the right. (Note that it is necessary to turn the pieces around so that the short sides are at the bottom in the arrangement lettered D. None of the other arrangements show pieces of the given size and shape.)

8.  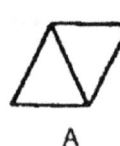      8.____

   A　　　　B　　　　C　　　　D

Questions 9-10.

DIRECTIONS: Questions 9 and 10 are questions designed to test your ability to identify forms of *Like* and *Unlike* proportions. In each of the questions, select from the drawings of objects labeled A, B, C, and D, the one that would have the TOP, Front, and Right views shown in the drawing at the left. Then, print the letter in the space at the right that has the same letter as your answer.

9. 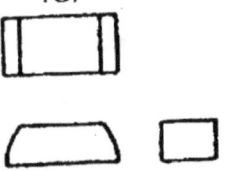  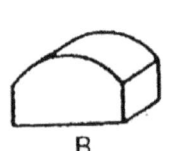  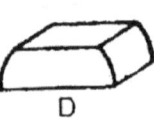   9.____

   FRONT  RIGHT    A           B           C           D

10. 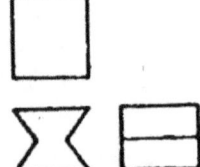   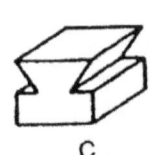    10.____

    FRONT  RIGHT    A           B           C           D

Questions 11-14.

Explanation and Commentary:
In each question, ONE rectangle is clearly wrong. For each question, use the measuring gage to check each of the rectangles and to find the WRONG one. Do this by putting the measuring gage rectangle on the question rectangle with the same letter so that the rectangles slightly overlap and the thin lines are parallel, like the one at the right. In this case, the height of the question rectangle exactly matches the height of the measuring gage rectangle, so the question rectangle is the right height.

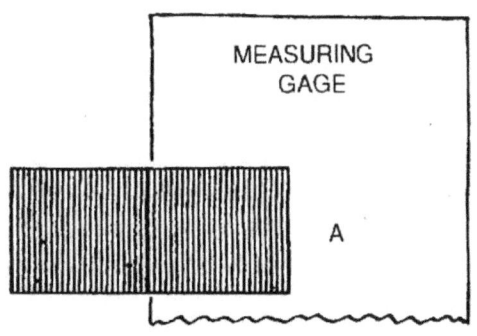

Once in every question when you put a measuring gage rectangle on a question rectangle, you will find that the heights do NOT match and that the question rectangle is clearly wrong, like the one at the right. In this case, you mark in the space at the right the same letter as the wrong rectangle. REMEMBER TO LINE UP THE MEASURING RECTANGLE WITH EACH QUESTION RECTANGLE SO THAT THE THIN LINES ARE EXACTLY PARALLEL.

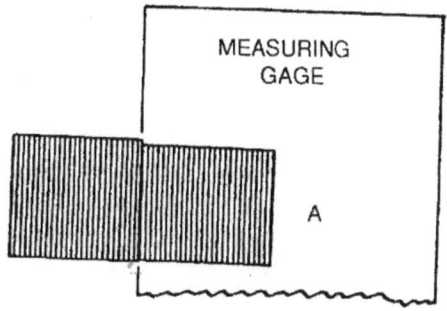

Now cut out the measuring gage on the last page and practice on the questions. The test will be limited, so practice doing them rapidly and accurately.

Questions 11 through 14 test how quickly and accurately you can check the heights of rectangles with a measuring gage. Each question has five rectangles of different heights. The height is the dimension that runs the same way as the thin lines.

11. _____
12. _____
13. _____
14. _____

## 4 (#1)

MEASURING GAGE

A

B

C

D

E

---

## KEY (CORRECT ANSWERS)

| | | | |
|---|---|---|---|
| 1. | B | 8. | B |
| 2. | B | 9. | D |
| 3. | C | 10. | B |
| 4. | A | 11. | D |
| 5. | E | 12. | C |
| 6. | E | 13. | B |
| 7. | D | 14. | A |

# EXAMINATION SECTION

## TEST 1

DIRECTIONS: Each question or incomplete statement is accompanied by figures or diagrams with two suggested answers. Select A or B if one of them BEST answers the question or completes the statement. If the two figures have the same value, choose answer C. *PRINT THE LETTER OF THE CORRECT ANSWER IN THE SPACE AT THE RIGHT.*

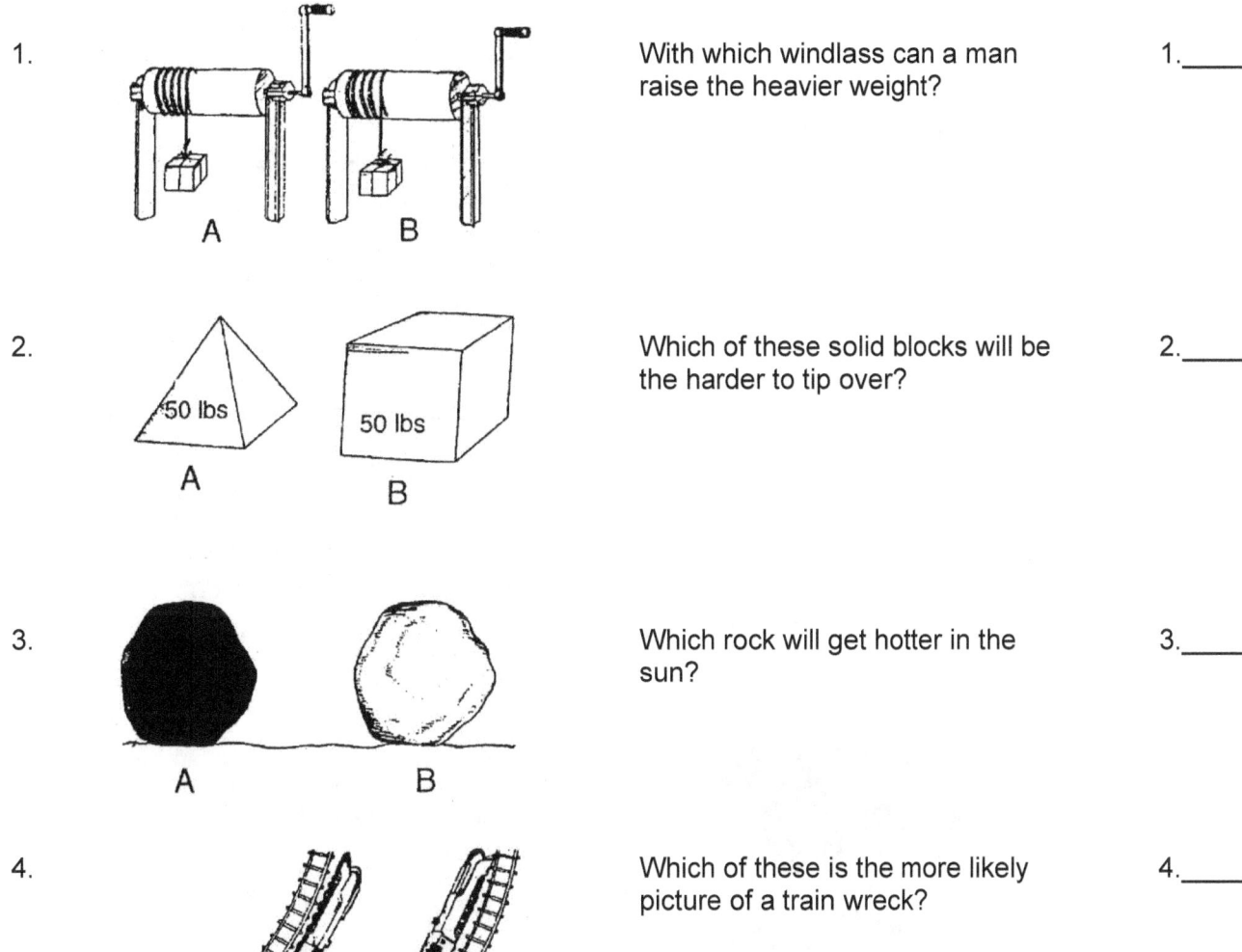

1. With which windlass can a man raise the heavier weight?   1.____

2. Which of these solid blocks will be the harder to tip over?   2.____

3. Which rock will get hotter in the sun?   3.____

4. Which of these is the more likely picture of a train wreck?   4.____

5. If the track is exactly level, on which rail does more pressure com? 5._____

6. Which picture shows the way a bomb falls from a moving airplane if there is no wind? 6._____

7. Indicate a gear which turn the same direction as the driver? 7._____

8. If there are no clouds, on which night will you be able to see more stars? 8._____

3 (#1)

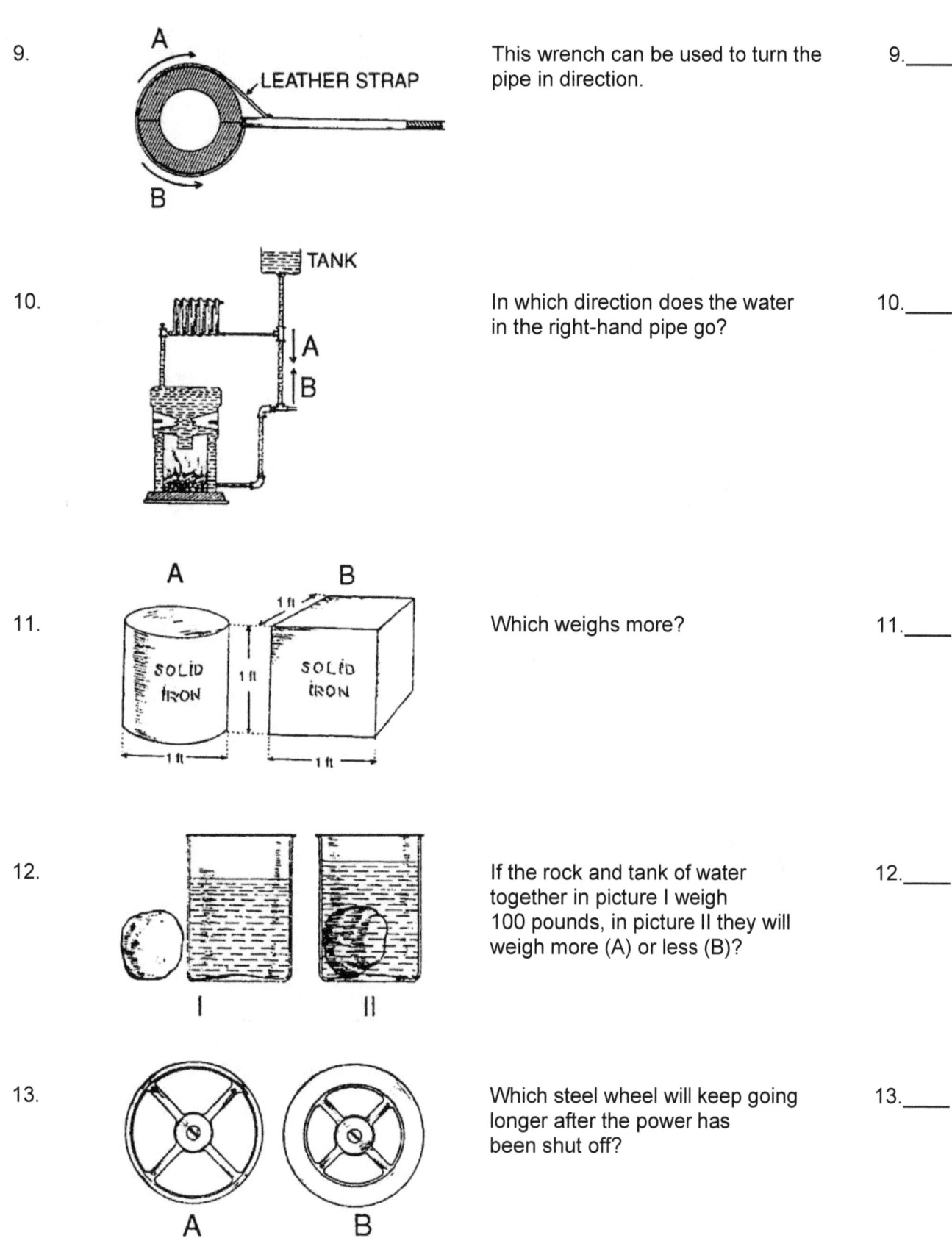

9. This wrench can be used to turn the pipe in direction.  9.____

10. In which direction does the water in the right-hand pipe go?  10.____

11. Which weighs more?  11.____

12. If the rock and tank of water together in picture I weigh 100 pounds, in picture II they will weigh more (A) or less (B)?  12.____

13. Which steel wheel will keep going longer after the power has been shut off?  13.____

14. 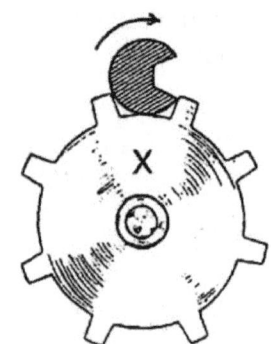 The top of the wheel X will go
    A. steadily to the right
    B. steadily to the left
    C. by jerks to the left

14.____

15. 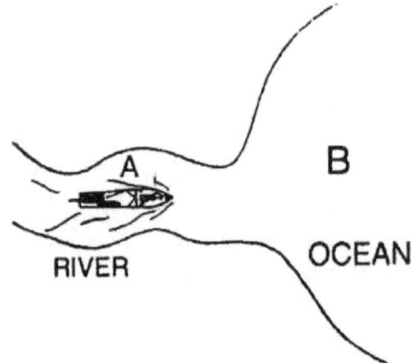 At which point will the boat be lower in the water?

15.____

16. 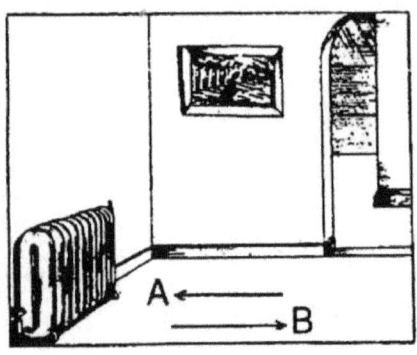 Which arrow shows the way the air will move along the floor when the radiator is turned on?

16.____

17. 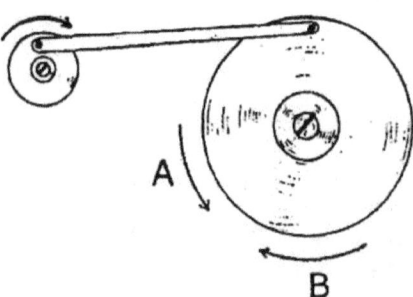 When the little wheel turns around, the big wheel will
    A. turn in direction A
    B. turn in direction B
    C. move back and forth

17.____

18. [50 WATT BULB A / 100 WATT BULB B] Which boy gets more light on the pages of his book? 18.____

19. [Milk A / Cream B] Which weighs more? 19.____

20. [coils A and B] Which of these wires offers more resistance to the passage of an electric current? 20.____

21. [wheel with spots A and B] Which spot on the wheel travels faster? 21.____

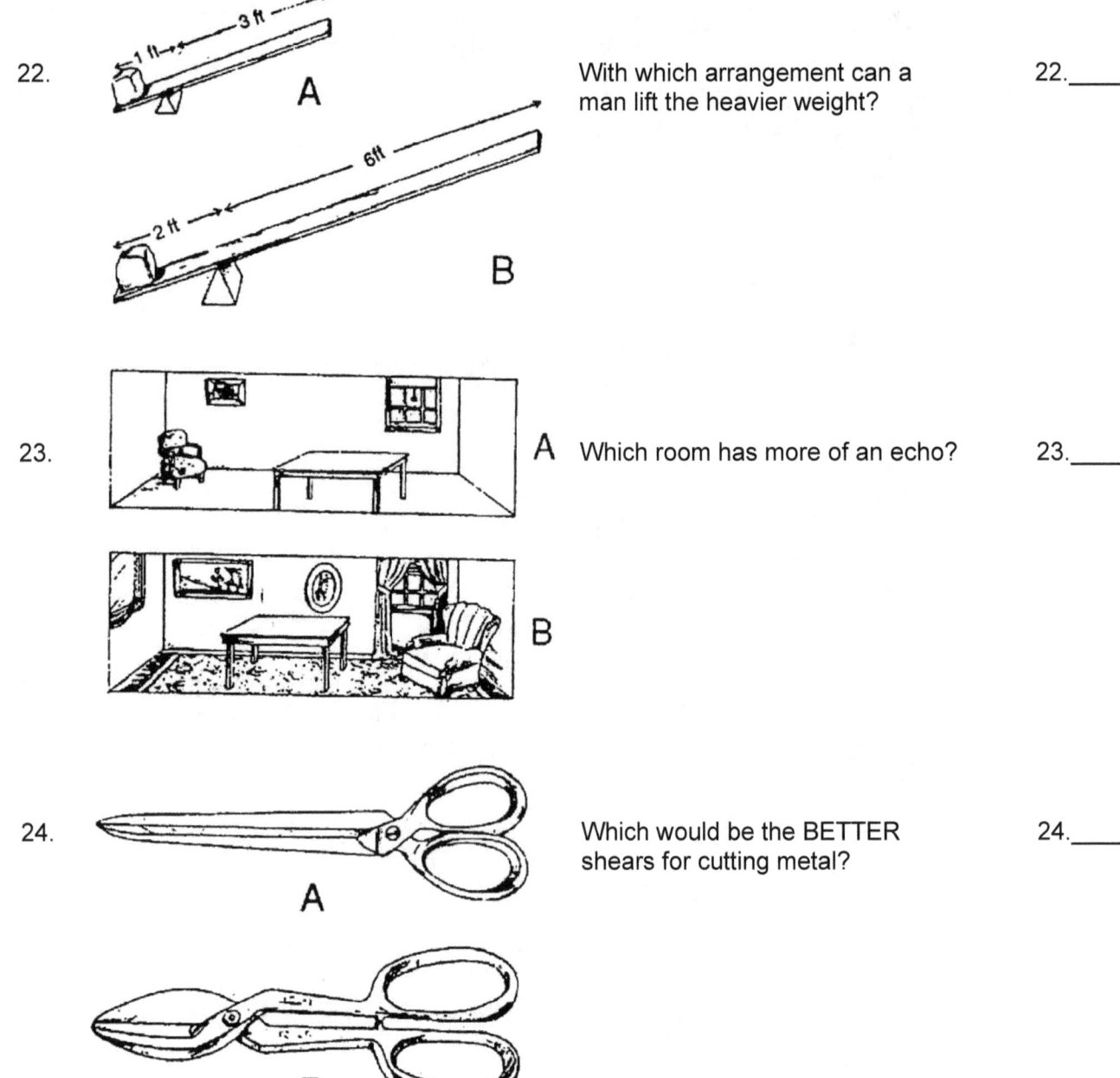

22. With which arrangement can a man lift the heavier weight?  22.____

23. Which room has more of an echo?  23.____

24. Which would be the BETTER shears for cutting metal?  24.____

## KEY (CORRECT ANSWERS)

| | | | |
|---|---|---|---|
| 1. | A | 11. | B |
| 2. | A | 12. | C |
| 3. | A | 13. | B |
| 4. | A | 14. | C |
| 5. | B | 15. | A |
| 6. | A | 16. | A |
| 7. | B | 17. | C |
| 8. | B | 18. | A |
| 9. | A | 19. | A |
| 10. | A | 20. | A |

21. B
22. B
23. A
24. B

# MECHANICAL APTITUDE
# MECHANICAL COMPREHENSION
# EXAMINATION SECTION
# TEST 1

DIRECTIONS: Each question or incomplete statement below is followed by several suggested answers or completions. Select the *one* that *BEST* answers the question or completes the statement. *PRINT THE LETTER OF THE CORRECT ANSWER IN THE SPACE AT THE RIGHT.*

Questions 1-3.

DIRECTIONS: Questions 1 to 3 inclusive are based upon the following paragraph.

The only openings permitted in fire partitions except openings for ventilating ducts shall be those required for doors. There shall be but one such door opening unless the provision of additional openings would not exceed, in total width of all doorways, 25 percent of the length of the wall. The minimum distance between openings shall be three feet. The maximum area for such a door opening shall be 80 square feet, except that such openings for the passage of motor trucks may be a maximum of 140 square feet.

1. According to the above paragraph, openings in fire partitions are permitted *only* for

   A. doors
   B. doors and windows
   C. doors and ventilation ducts
   D. doors, windows and ventilation ducts

2. In a fire partition, 22 feet long and 10 feet high, the MAXIMUM number of doors, 3 feet wide and 7 feet high, is

   A. 1      B. 2      C. 3      D. 4

3. 

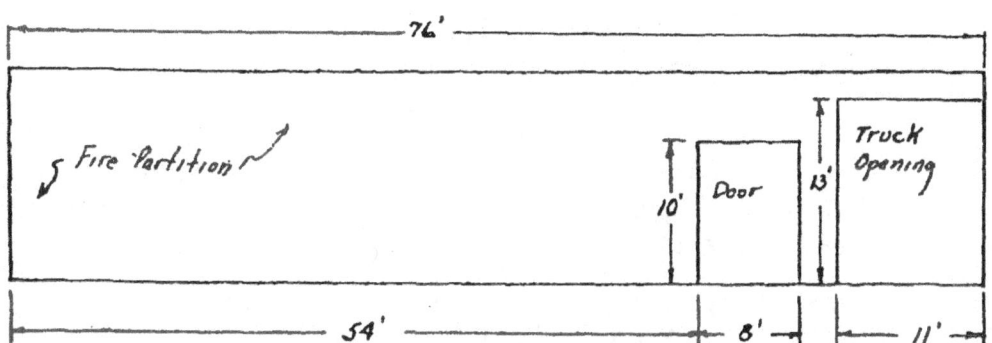

The one of the following statements about the layout shown above that is MOST accurate is that the

   A. total width of the openings is too large
   B. truck opening is too large
   C. truck and door openings are too close together
   D. layout is acceptable

17

4. At a given temperature, a wet hand will freeze to a bar of metal, but NOT to a piece of wood, because the

   A. metal expands and contracts more than the wood
   B. wood is softer than the metal
   C. wood will burn at a lower temperature than the metal
   D. metal is a better conductor of heat than the wood

5. Of the following items commonly found in a household, the one that uses the MOST electric current is a(n)

   A. 150-watt light bulb
   B. toaster
   C. door buzzer
   D. 8" electric fan

6. Sand and ashes are frequently placed on icy pavements to prevent skidding. The effect of the sand and ashes is to increase

   A. inertia
   B. gravity
   C. momentum
   D. friction

7. The air near the ceiling of a room usually is warmer than the air near the floor because

   A. there is better air circulation at the floor level
   B. warm air is lighter than cold air
   C. windows usually are nearer the floor than the ceiling
   D. heating pipes usually run along the ceiling

8. 

DIA. 1        DIA. 2

It is safer to use the ladder positioned as shown in diagram 1 than as shown in diagram 2 because, in diagram 1,

   A. less strain is placed upon the center rungs of the ladder
   B. it is easier to grip and stand on the ladder
   C. the ladder reaches a lower height
   D. the ladder is less likely to tip over backwards

9.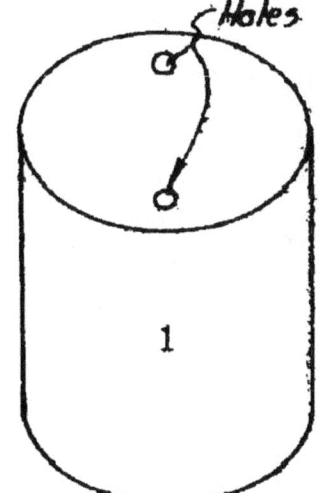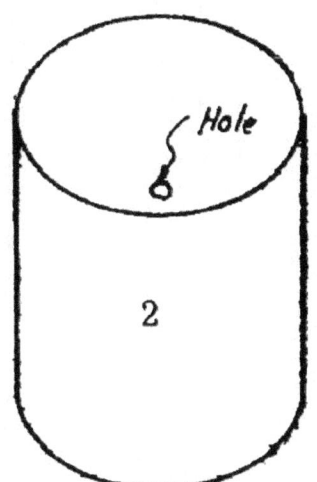

It is *easier* to pour a liquid from:

A. Can 1 because there are two holes from which the liquid can flow
B. Can 1 because air can enter through one hole while the liquid comes out the other hole
C. Can 2 because the liquid comes out under greater pressure
D. Can 2 because it is easier to direct the flow of the liquid when there is only one hole

10. A substance which is subject to "spontaneous combustion" is one that

A. is explosive when heated
B. is capable of catching fire without an external source of heat
C. acts to speed up the burning of material
D. liberates oxygen when heated

11. The sudden shutting down of a nozzle on a hose discharging water under high pressure is a *bad* practice *CHIEFLY* because the

A. hose is likely to whip about violently
B. hose is likely to burst
C. valve handle is likely to snap
D. valve handle is likely to jam

12. Fire can continue where there are present fuel, oxygen from the air or other source, and a sufficiently high temperature to maintain combustion. The method of extinguishment of fire *MOST* commonly used is to

A. remove the fuel
B. exclude the oxygen from the burning material
C. reduce the temperature of the burning material
D. smother the flames of the burning material

13.

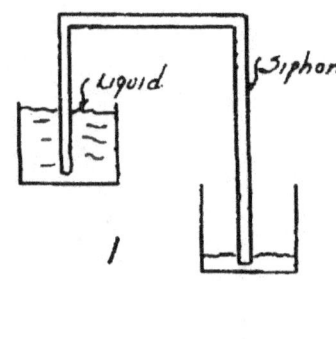
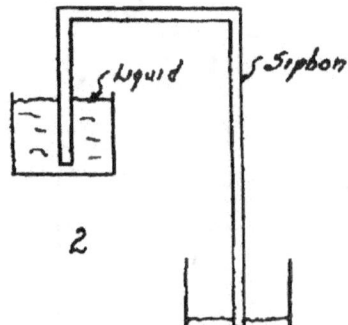
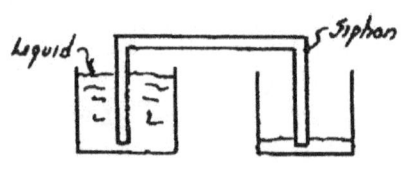
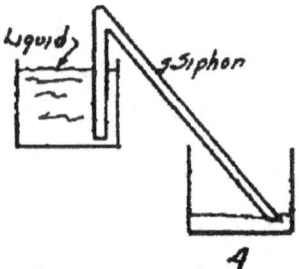

The *one* of the siphon arrangements shown above which would MOST quickly transfer a solution from the container on the left side to the one on the right side is numbered

A. 1  B. 2  C. 3  D. 4

14. Static electricity is a hazard in industry CHIEFLY because it may cause

A. dangerous or painful burns
B. chemical decomposition of toxic elements
C. sparks which can start an explosion
D. overheating of electrical equipment

15.

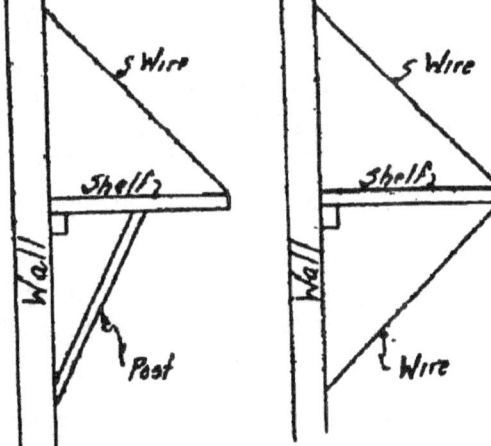

The STRONGEST method of supporting the shelf is shown in diagram

A. 1  B. 2  C. 3  D. 4

16. A row boat will float *deeper* in fresh water than in salt water *because*  16____

    A. in the salt water the salt will occupy part of the space
    B. fresh water is heavier than salt water
    C. salt water is heavier than fresh water
    D. salt water offers less resistance than fresh water

17.  17____

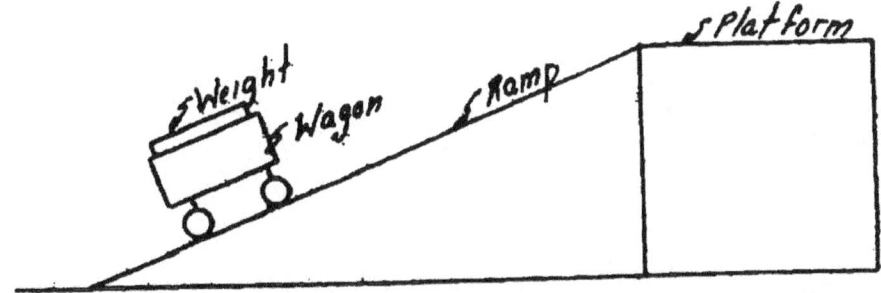

It is easier to get the load onto the platform by using the ramp than it is to lift it directly onto the platform. This is *true* because the effect of the ramp is to

    A. reduce the amount of friction so that less force is required
    B. distribute the weight over a larger area
    C. support part of the load so that less force is needed to move the wagon
    D. increase the effect of the moving weight

18.  18____

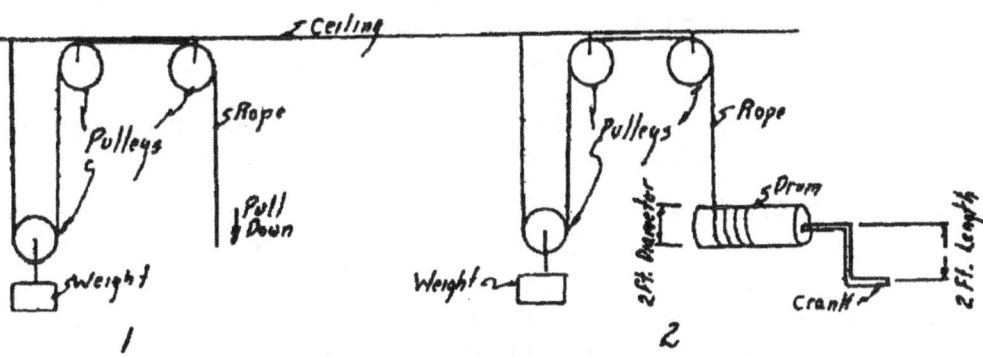

More weight can be lifted by the method shown in diagram 2 than as shown in diagram 1 because

    A. it takes less force to turn a crank than it does to pull in a straight line
    B. the drum will prevent the weight from falling by itself
    C. the length of the crank is larger than the radius of the drum
    D. the drum has more rope on it easing the pull

19.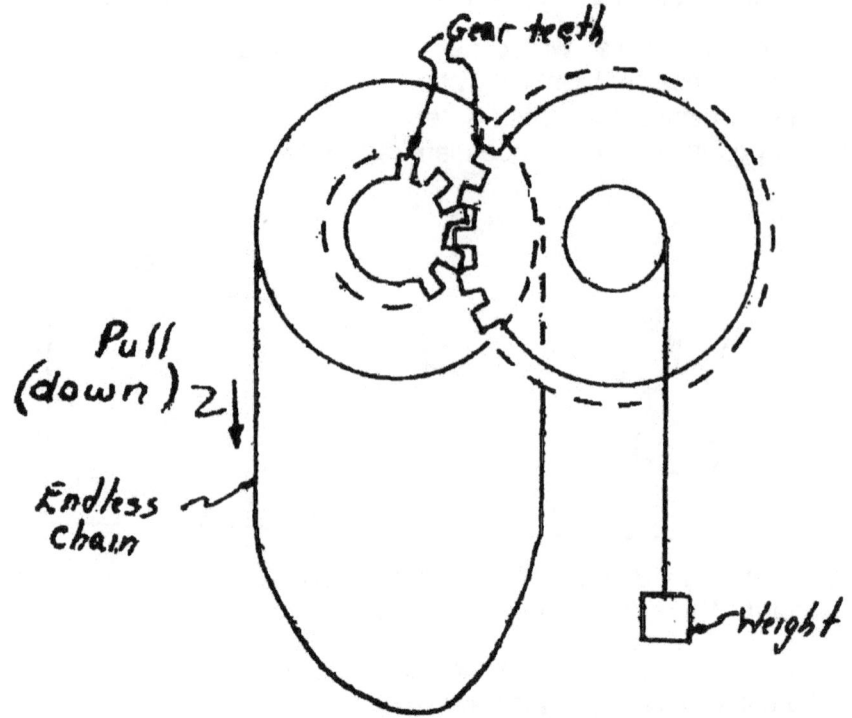

As the endless chain is pulled down in the direction shown, the weight will move

- A. *up* faster than the endless chain is pulled down
- B. *up* slower than the endless chain is pulled down
- C. *down* faster than the endless chain is pulled down
- D. *down* slower than the endless chain is pulled down

20. Two balls of the same size, but different weights, are both dropped from a 10-ft. height. The one of the following statements that is MOST accurate is that

- A. both balls will reach the ground at the same time because they are the same size
- B. both balls will reach the ground at the same time because the effect of gravity is the same on both balls
- C. the heavier ball will reach the ground first because it weighs more
- D. the lighter ball will reach the ground first because air resistance is greater on the heavier ball

21. It is considered poor practice to increase the leverage of a wrench by placing a pipe over the handle of the wrench. This is true PRINCIPALLY because

- A. the wrench may break
- B. the wrench may slip off the nut
- C. it is harder to place the wrench on the nut
- D. the wrench is more difficult to handle

22.

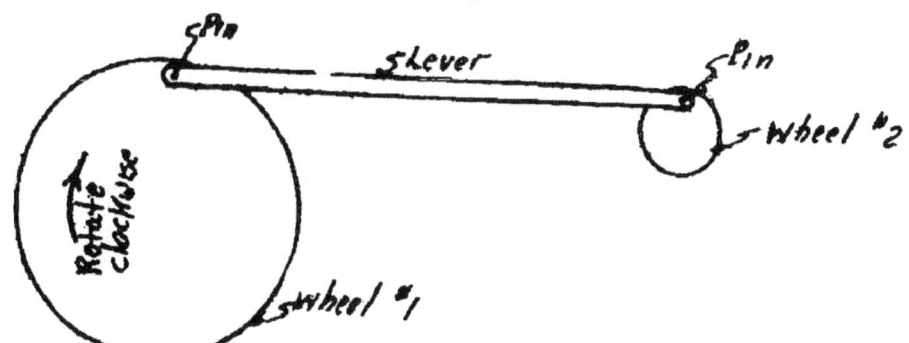

If wheel #1 is turned in the direction shown, wheel #2 will

- A. turn continously in a clockwise direction
- B. turn continously in a counterclockwise direction
- C. move back and fourth
- D. became jammed and both wheels will shop

23. ALL SOLID AREAS REPRESENT EQUAL WEIGHTS ATTACHED TO THE FLYWHEEL

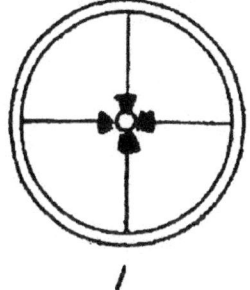 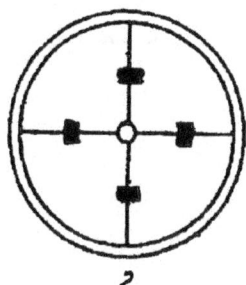 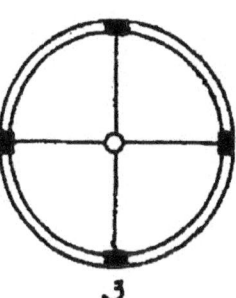

The above diagrams are of flywheels made of the same material with the same dimensions and attached to similar engines. The solid areas represent equal weights attached to the fly wheel. If all three engines are running at the same speed for the same length of time and the power to the engines is shut of simultaneously,

- A. wheel 1 will continue turning longest
- B. wheel 2 will continue turning longest
- C. wheel 3 will continue turning longest
- D. all three wheels will continue turning for the same time

24. The one of the following substance which expands when freezing is

A. alcohol   B. ammonia   C. mercury   D. water

25. A piece of copper wire 30 feet long is cut into two pieces, 20 feet and 10 feet. The resistance of the *longer* piece, compared to the shorter, is

- A. one-half as much
- B. two-thirds as much
- C. one and one-half as much
- D. twice as much

## KEY (CORRECT ANSWERS)

1. C
2. A
3. B
4. D
5. B

6. D
7. B
8. D
9. B
10. B

11. B
12. C
13. B
14. C
15. A

16. C
17. C
18. C
19. D
20. B

21. A
22. D
23. C
24. D
25. D

# TEST 2

DIRECTIONS: Each question or incomplete statement below is followed by several suggested answers or completions. Select the *one* that BEST answers the question or completes the statement. *PRINT THE LETTER OF THE CORRECT ANSWER IN THE SPACE AT THE RIGHT.*

Questions 1-2.

DIRECTIONS: Questions 1 and 2 are to be answered in accordance with the information in the following statement:

The electrical resistance of copper wires varies directly with their lengths and inversely with their cross section areas.

1. A piece of copper wire 30 feet long is cut into two pieces, 20 feet and 10 feet. The resistance of the *longer* piece, compared to the shorter, is

   A. one-half as much
   B. two-thirds as much
   C. one and one-half as much
   D. twice as much

   1___

2. Two pieces of copper wire are each 10 feet long but the cross section area of one is 2/3 that of the other. The resistance of the piece with the *larger* cross-section area is

   A. one-half the resistance of the smaller
   B. two-thirds the resistance of the smaller
   C. one and one-half times the resistance of the smaller
   D. twice the resistance of the smaller

   2___

3. 

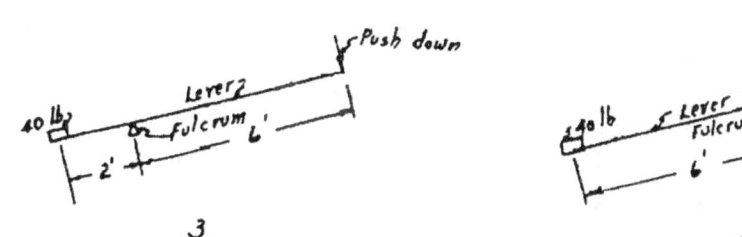

The arrangement of the lever which would require the LEAST amount of force to move the weight is shown in the diagram numbered

   A. 1    B. 2    C. 3    D. 4

   3___

4. Steel supporting beams in buildings often are surrounded by a thin layer of concrete to keep the beams from becoming hot and collapsing during a fire.
The *one* of the following statements which BEST explains how collapse is prevented by this arrangement is that concrete

   A. becomes stronger as its temperature is increased

   4___

25

B. acts as an insulating material
C. protects the beam from rust and corrosion
D. reacts chemically with steel at high temperatures

5. If boiling water is poured into a drinking glass, the glass is likely to crack. If, however, a metal spoon first is placed in the glass, it is much less likely to crack. The reason that the glass with the spoon is *less likely* to crack is that the spoon

   A. distributes the water over a larger surface of the glass
   B. quickly absorbs heat from the water
   C. reinforces the glass
   D. reduces the amount of water which can be poured into the glass

6. It takes *more* energy to force water through a *long* pipe than through a *short* pipe of the same diameter. The PRINCIPAL reason for this is

   A. gravity    B. friction    C. inertia    D. cohesion

7. A pump, discharging at 300 lbs.-per-sq.-inch pressure, delivers water through 100 feet of pipe laid horizontally. If the valve at the end of the pipe is shut so that no water can flow, then the pressure at the valve is, for practical purposes,

   A. *greater* than the pressure at the pump
   B. *equal to* the pressure at the pump
   C. *less* than the pressure at the pump
   D. *greater or less* than the pressure at the pump, depending on the type of pump used

8. The explosive force of a gas when stored under various pressures is given in the following table:

   | Storage Pressure | Explosive Force |
   | --- | --- |
   | 10 | 1 |
   | 20 | 8 |
   | 30 | 27 |
   | 40 | 64 |
   | 50 | 125 |

   The *one* of the following statements which BEST expresses the relationship between the storage pressure and explosive force is that
   A. there is no systematic relationship between an increase in storage pressure and an increase in explosive force
   B. the explosive force varies as the square of the pressure
   C. the explosive force varies as the cube of the pressure
   D. the explosive force varies as the fourth power of the pressure

9.

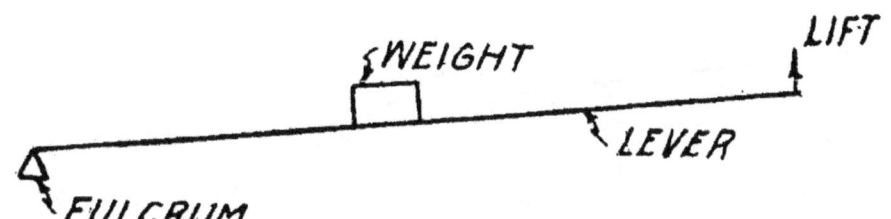

The leverage system in the sketch above is used to raise a weight. In order to *reduce* the amount of force required to raise the weight, it is necessary to

A. decrease the length of the lever
B. place the weight closer to the fulcrum
C. move the weight closer to the person applying the force
D. move the fulcrum further from the weight

10. In the accompanying sketch of a block and fall, if the end of the rope P is pulled so that it moves one foot, the distance the weight will be *raised* is
A. 1/2 ft.
B. 1 ft.
C. 1 1/2 ft.
D. 2 ft.

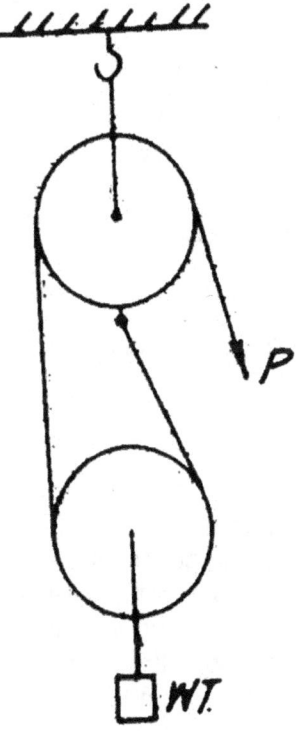

11.

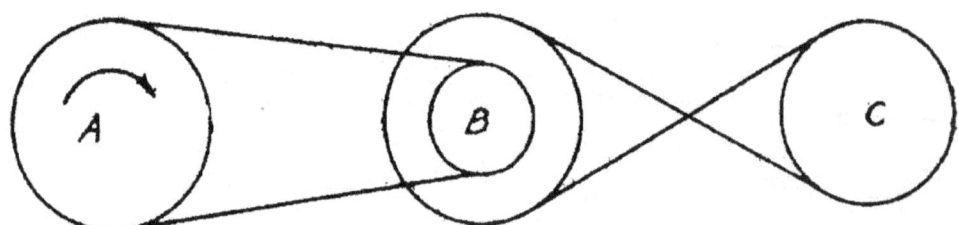

The above sketch diagrammatically shows a pulley and belt system. If pulley A is made to rotate in a clockwise direction, *then* pulley C will rotate

A. faster than pulley A and in a clockwise direction
B. slower than pulley A and in a clockwise direction
C. faster than pulley A and in a counter-clockwise direction
D. slower than pulley A and in a counter-clockwise direction

12.

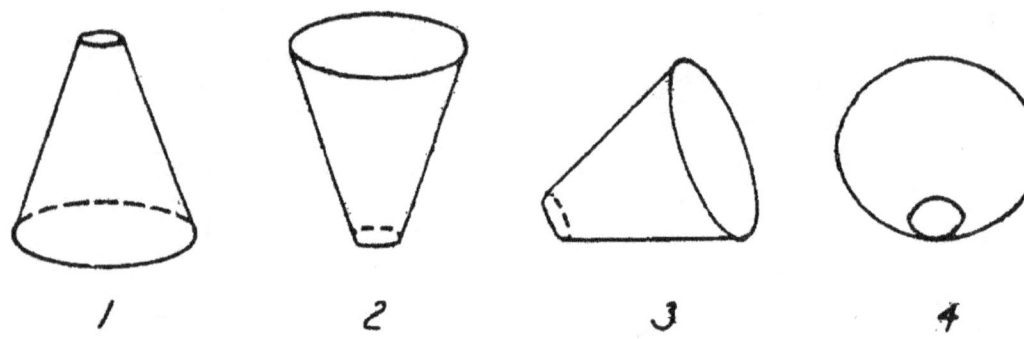

The above diagrams show four positions of the same object. The position in which this object is MOST stable is

A. 1      B. 2      C. 3      D. 4

13. The accompanying sketch diagrammatically shows a system of meshing gears with relative diameters as drawn. If gear 1 is made to rotate in the direction of the arrow, *then* the gear that will turn *FASTEST* is numbered

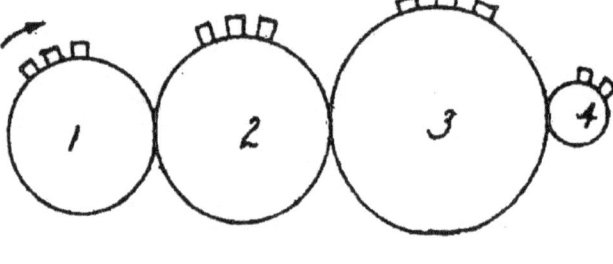

A. 1      B. 2      C. 3      D. 4

14.

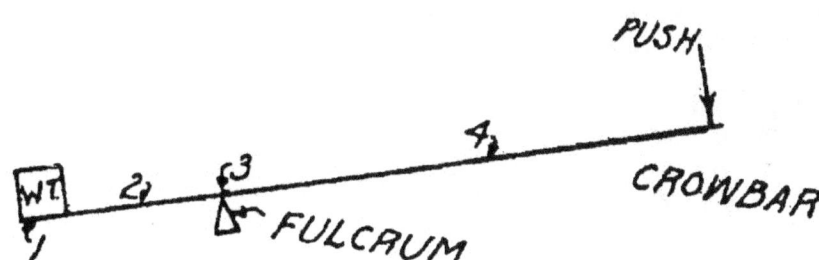

The above sketch shows a weight being lifted by means of a crowbar.
The point at which the tendency for the bar to break is *GREATEST* is

A. 1   B. 2   C. 3   D. 4

15.

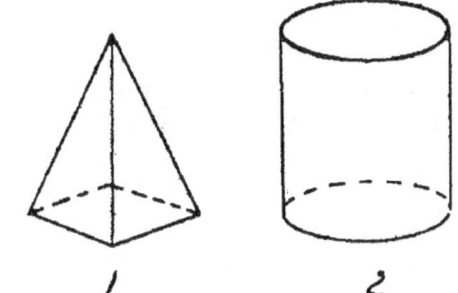

The above sketches show four objects which weigh the same but have different shapes.
The object which is *MOST* difficult to tip over is numbered

A. 1   B. 2   C. 3   D. 4

16.

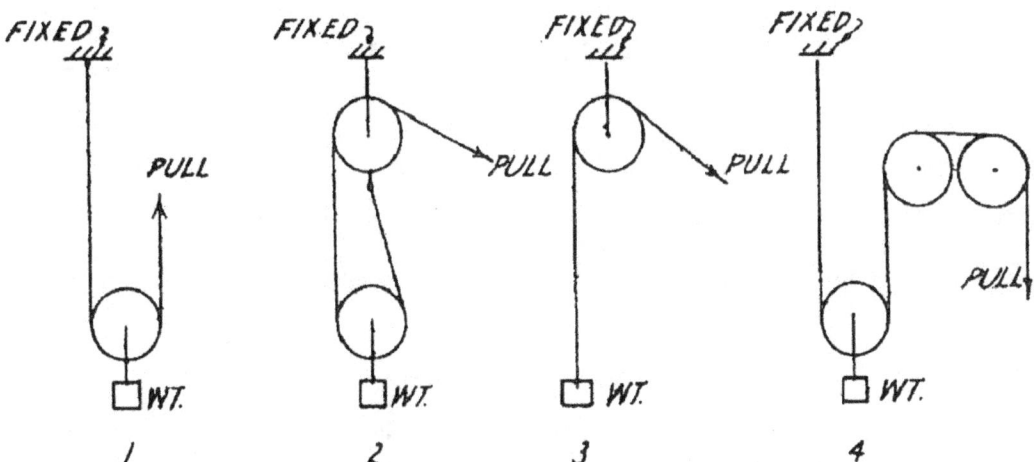

An object is to be lifted by means of a system of lines and pulleys. Of the systems shown above, the *one* which would require the *GREATEST* force to be used in lifting the weight is the one numbered

A. 1   B. 2   C. 3   D. 4

17. An intense fire develops in a room in which carbon dioxide cylinders are stored. The PRINCIPAL hazard in this situation is that

    A. the $CO_2$ may catch fire
    B. toxic fumes may be released
    C. the cylinders may explode
    D. released $CO_2$ may intensify the fire

18. At a fire involving the roof of a 5-story building, the firemen trained their hose stream on the fire from a vacant lot across the street, aiming the stream at a point about 15 feet above the roof.
    In this situation, water in the stream would be traveling at the GREATEST speed

    A. as it leaves the hose nozzle
    B. at a point midway between the ground and the roof
    C. at the maximum height of the stream
    D. as it drops on the roof

19. A principle of lighting is that the intensity of illumination at a point is inversely proportional to the square of the distance from the source of illumination.
    Assume that a pulley lamp is lowered from a position of 6 feet to one of three feet above a desk. According to the above principle, we would expect that the amount of illumination reaching the desk from the lamp in the lower position, as compared to the higher position, will be

    A. half as much  B. twice as much
    C. four times as much  D. nine times as much

20.

    1   2   3   4

    When standpipes are required in a structure, sufficient risers must be installed so that no point on the floor is more than 120 feet from a riser.
    The one of the above diagrams which gives the MAXIMUM area which can be covered by one riser is

    A. 1   B. 2   C. 3   D. 4

21. Spontaneous combustion may be the reason for a pile of oily rags catching fire. In general, spontaneous combustion is the DIRECT result of

    A. application of flame   B. falling sparks
    C. intense sunlight       D. chemical action
    E. radioactivity

22. In general, firemen are advised not to direct a solid stream of water on fires burning in electrical equipment. Of the following, the MOST logical reason for this instruction is that

    A. water is a conductor of electricity
    B. water will do more damage to the electrical equipment than the fire
    C. hydrogen in water may explode when it comes in contact with electric current
    D. water will not effectively extinguish fires in electrical equipment
    E. water may spread the fire to other circuits

23. The height at which a fireboat will float in still water is determined CHIEFLY by the

    A. weight of the water displaced by the boat
    B. horsepower of the boat's engines
    C. number of propellers on the boat
    D. curve the bow has above the water line
    E. skill with which the boat is maneuvered

24. When firemen are working at the nozzle of a hose they usually lean forward on the hose. The most likely reason for taking this position is that

    A. the surrounding air is cooled, making the firemen more comfortable
    B. a backward force is developed which must be counteracted
    C. the firemen can better see where the stream strikes
    D. the fireman are better protected from injury by falling debris
    E. the stream is projected further

25. In general, the color and odor of smoke will BEST indicate

    A. the cause of the fire
    B. the extent of the fire
    C. how long the fire has been burning
    D. the kind of material on fire
    E. the exact seat of the fire

## KEY (CORRECT ANSWERS)

1. D
2. B
3. A
4. B
5. B

6. B
7. B
8. C
9. B
10. A

11. C
12. A
13. D
14. C
15. A

16. C
17. C
18. A
19. C
20. C

21. D
22. A
23. A
24. B
25. D

# TEST 3

DIRECTIONS: Each question or incomplete statement below is followed by several suggested answers or completions. Select the *one* that *BEST* answers the question or completes the statement. *PRINT THE LETTER OF THE CORRECT ANSWER IN THE SPACE AT THE RIGHT.*

1. As a demonstration, firemen set up two hose lines identical in every respect except that one was longer than the other. Water was then delivered through these lines from one pump and it was seen that the stream from the longer hose line had a shorter "throw," Of the following, the *MOST* valid explanation of this difference in "throw" is that the

    A. air resistance to the water stream is proportional to the length of hose
    B. time required for water to travel through the longer hose is greater than for the shorter one
    C. loss due to friction is greater in the longer hose than in the shorter one
    D. rise of temperature is greater in the longer hose than in the shorter one
    E. longer hose line probably developed a leak at one of the coupling joints

    1____

2. Of the following toxic gases, the *one* which is *MOST* dangerous because it cannot be seen and has no odor, is

    A. ether  B. carbon monoxide  C. chlorine
    D. ammonia  E. cooking gas

    2____

3. You are visiting with some friends when their young son rushes into the room with his clothes on fire. You immediately wrap him in a rug and roll him on the floor. The *MOST* important reason for your action is that the

    A. flames are confined within the rug
    B. air supply to the fire is reduced
    C. burns sustained will be third degree, rather than first degree
    D. whirling action will put out the fire
    E. boy will not suffer from shock

    3____

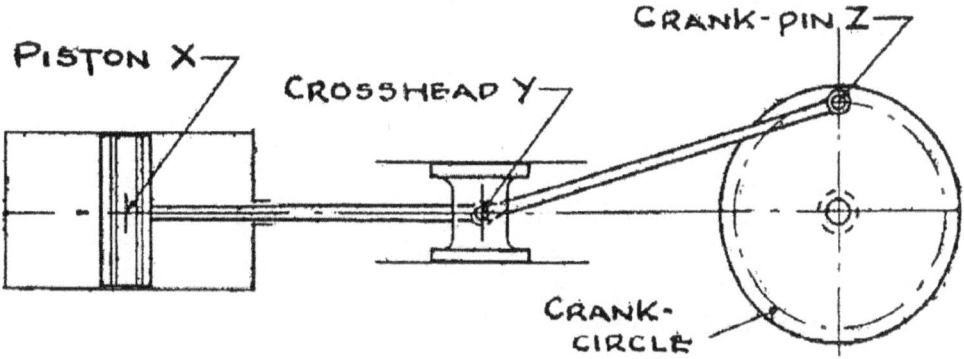

FIGURE I

33

Questions 4-6,

DIRECTIONS: The device shown in Figure I above represents schematically a mechanism commonly used to change reciprocating (back and forth) motion to rotation (circular) motion.
The following questions, numbered 4 to 6 inclusive, are to be answered with reference to this device.

4. Assume that piston X is placed in its extreme left position so that X, Y and Z are in a horizontal line. If a horizontal force to the right is applied to the piston X, we may then expect that

    A. the crank-pin Z will revolve clockwise
    B. the crosshead Y will move in a direction opposite to that of X
    C. the crank-pin Z will revolve counterclockwise
    D. no movement will take place
    E. the crank-pin Z will oscillate back and forth

4_____

5. If we start from the position shown in the above diagram, and move piston X to the right, the result will be that

    A. the crank-pin Z will revolve counterclockwise and cross-head Y will move to the left
    B. the crank-pin Z will revolve clockwise and crosshead Y will move to the left
    C. the crank-pin Z will revolve clockwise and crosshead Y will move to the right
    D. the crank-pin Z will revolve clockwise and crosshead Y will move to the right
    E. crosshead Y will move to the left as piston X moves to the right

5_____

6. If crank-pin Z is moved closer to the center of the crank circle, then the length of the

    A. stroke of piston X is increased
    B. stroke of piston X is decreased
    C. stroke of piston X is unchanged
    D. rod between the piston X and crosshead Y is increased
    E. rod between the piston X and crosshead Y is decreased

6_____

Questions 7-8.

DIRECTIONS: Figure II represents schematically a block-and-fall tackle. The advantage derived from this machine is that the effect of the applied force is multiplied by the number of lines of rope directly supporting the load. The following two questions, numbered 7 and 8, are to be answered with reference to this figure.

7. Pull P is exerted on line T to raise the load L. The line in which the *LARGEST* strain is finally induced is line

    A. T        B. U        C. V        D. X        E. Y

7_____

8. If the largest pull P that two men can apply to line T is 280 lbs., the *MAXIMUM* load L that they can raise without regard to frictional losses is, *most nearly*, _____ lbs.
   A. 1960
   B. 1680
   C. 1400
   D. 1260
   E. 1120

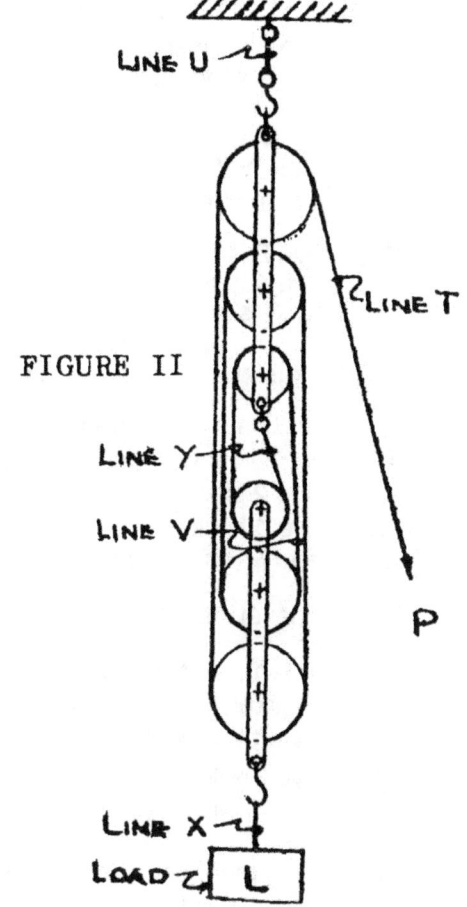

FIGURE II

Questions 9-13.

DIRECTIONS: Answer Questions 9 to 13 on the basis of Figure III. The diagram schematically illustrates part of a water tank. 1 and 5 are outlet and inlet pipes, respectively. 2 is a valve which can be used to open and close the outlet pipe by hand. 3 is a float which is rigidly connected to valve 4 by an iron bar, thus causing that valve to open or shut as the float rises or falls 4 is a hinged valve which controls the flow of water into the tank.

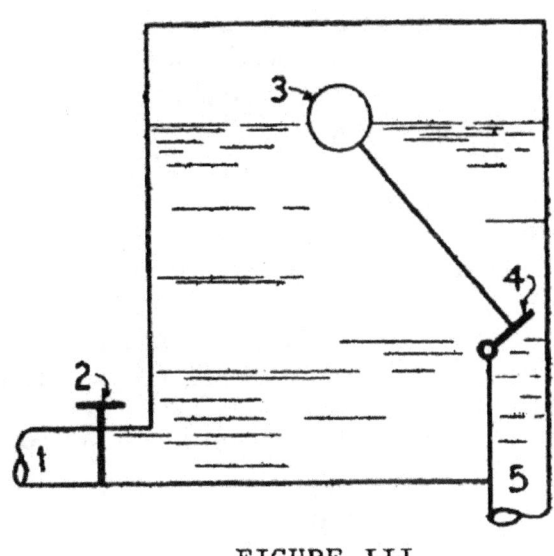

FIGURE III

9. If the tank is half filled and water is going out of pipe 1 more rapidly than it is coming in through pipe 5, *then*

    A. valve 2 is closed
    B. float 3 is rising in the tank
    C. valve 4 is opening wider
    D. valve 4 is closed
    E. float 3 is stationary

10. If the tank is half filled with water and water is coming in through inlet pipe 5 more rapidly than it is going out through outlet pipe 1, *then*

    A. valve 2 is closed
    B. float 3 is rising in the tank
    C. valve 4 is opening wider
    D. valve 4 is closed
    E. float 3 is stationary

11. If the tank is empty, then it can *normally* be expected that

    A. float 3 is at its highest position
    B. float 3 is at its lowest position
    C. valve 2 is closed
    D. valve 4 is closed
    E. water will not come into the tank

12. If float 3 develops a leak, *then*

    A. the tank will tend to empty
    B. water will tend to stop coming into the tank
    C. valve 4 will tend to close
    D. valve 2 will tend to close
    E. valve 4 will tend to remain open

13. Without any other changes being made, if the bar joining the float to valve 4 is removed and a slightly shorter bar substituted, *then*

    A. a smaller quantity of water in the tank will be required before the float closes valve 4
    B. valve 4 will not open
    C. valve 4 will not close
    D. it is not possible to determine what will happen
    E. a greater quantity of water in the tank will be required before the float closes valve 4

Questions 14-18.

DIRECTIONS: Answer Questions 14 to 18 on the basis of Figure IV. A, B, C and D are four meshed gears forming a gear train. Gear A is the driver. Gears A and D each have twice as many teeth as gear B, and gear C has four times as many teeth as gear B. The diagram is schematic: the teeth go all around each gear.

14. *Two* gears which turn in the *same* direction are:

    A. A and B
    B. B and C
    C. C and D
    D. D and A
    E. B and D

15. The *two* gears which revolve at the *same* speed are gears

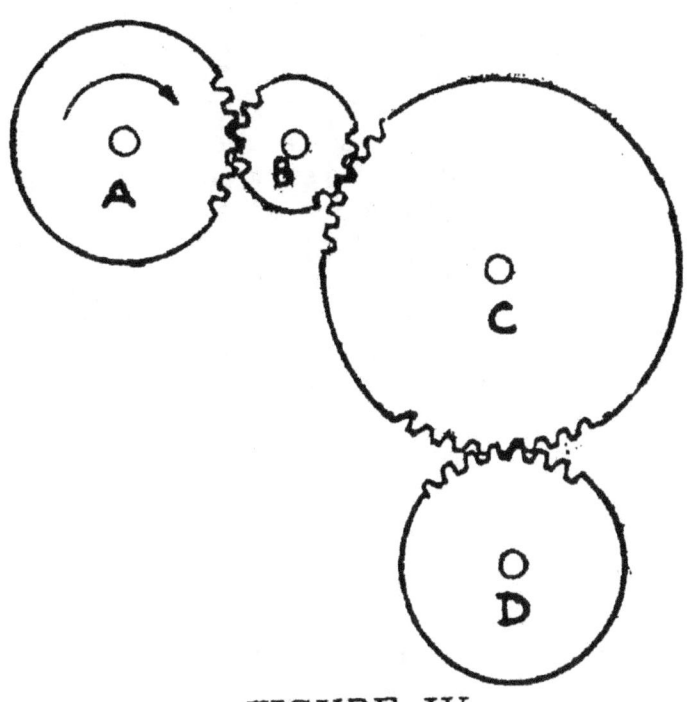

FIGURE IV

   A. A and C   B. A and D   C. B and C
   D. B and D   E. D and C

16. If all the teeth on gear C are stripped without affecting the teeth on gears A, B, and D, then rotation would occur *only* in gear(s)

   A. C   B. D   C. A and B
   D. A, B, and D   E. B and D

17. If gear D is rotating at the rate of 100 RPM, then gear B is rotating at the rate of _____ RPM.

   A. 25   B. 50   C. 100   D. 200   E. 400

18. If gear A turns at the rate of two revolutions per second, then the number of revolutions per second that gear C turns is

   A. 1   B. 2   C. 3   D. 4   E. 8

Questions 19-23.

DIRECTIONS: Answer Questions 19 to 23 on the basis of Figure V. The diagram shows a water pump in cross section: 1 is a check valve, 2 and 3 are the spring and diaphragm, respectively, of the discharge valve, 4 is the pump piston; 5 is the inlet valve, and 6 is the pump cylinder. All valves permit the flow of water in one direction only.

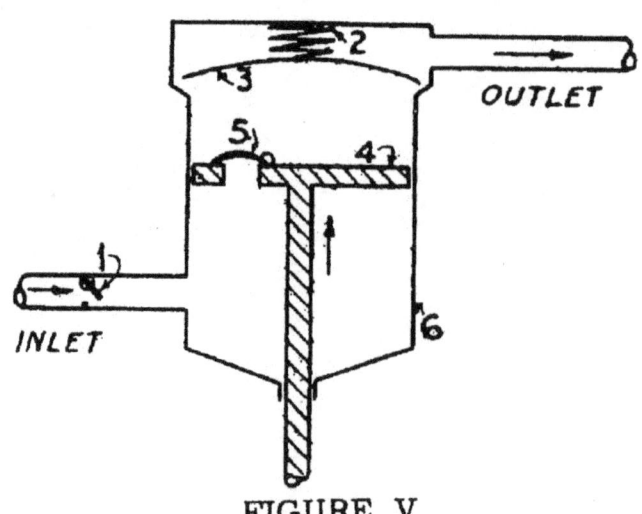

FIGURE V

19. When water is flowing through the outlet pipe,

    A. check valve 1 is closed
    B. diaphragm 3 is closed
    C. valve 5 is closed
    D. spring 2 is fully extended
    E. the piston is on the downstroke

20. If valve 5 does not work properly and stays closed, *then*

    A. the piston cannot move down
    B. the piston cannot move up
    C. diaphragm 3 cannot open
    D. check valve 1 cannot close
    E. the flow of water will be reversed

21. If diaphragm 3 does not work properly and stays in the open position, *then*

    A. check valve 1 will not open
    B. valve 5 will not open
    C. spring 2 will be compressed
    D. spring 2 will be extended
    E. water will not flow through the inlet pipe

22. When valve 5 is open during normal operation of the pump, *then*

    A. spring 2 is fully compressed
    B. the piston is on the upstroke
    C. water is flowing through check valve 1
    D. a vacuum is formed between the piston and the bottom of the cylinder
    E. diaphragm 3 is closed

23. If check valve 1 jams and stays closed, *then*

    A. valve 5 will be open on both the upstroke and down stroke of the piston
    B. a vacuum will tend to form in the inlet pipe between the source of the water supply and check valve 1
    C. pressure on the cylinder side of check valve 1 will increase

D. less force will be required to move the piston down
E. more force will be required to move the piston down

24. The one of the following which *BEST* explains why smoke usually rises from a fire is that   24____

    A. cooler, heavier air displaces lighter, warm air
    B. heat energy of the fire propels the smoke upward
    C. suction from the upper air pulls the smoke upward
    D. burning matter is chemically changed into heat energy

25. The practice of racing a car engine to warm it up in cold weather, generally, is   25____

    A. *good, MAINLY* because repeated stalling of the engine and drain on the battery is avoided
    B. *bad, MAINLY* because too much gas is used to get the engine heated
    C. *good, MAINLY* because the engine becomes operational in the shortest period of time
    D. *bad, MAINLY* because proper lubrication is not established rapidly enough

---

## KEY (CORRECT ANSWERS)

| | | | |
|---|---|---|---|
| 1. | C | 11. | B |
| 2. | B | 12. | E |
| 3. | B | 13. | A |
| 4. | D | 14. | E |
| 5. | D | 15. | B |
| 6. | B | 16. | C |
| 7. | B | 17. | D |
| 8. | B | 18. | A |
| 9. | C | 19. | C |
| 10. | B | 20. | A |

| | |
|---|---|
| 21. | C |
| 22. | E |
| 23. | D |
| 24. | A |
| 25. | D |

---

# MECHANICAL APTITUDE
# TEST OF MECHANICAL COMPREHENSION

INTRODUCTION: Look at Sample X on this page. It shows pictures of two rooms and asks, "Which room has more of an echo?" Because it has neither rugs nor curtains, there is more of an echo in Room "A"; so print the letter A in the space at the right. Now look at Sample Y and answer it yourself.

X    Which room has more of an echo?    X____

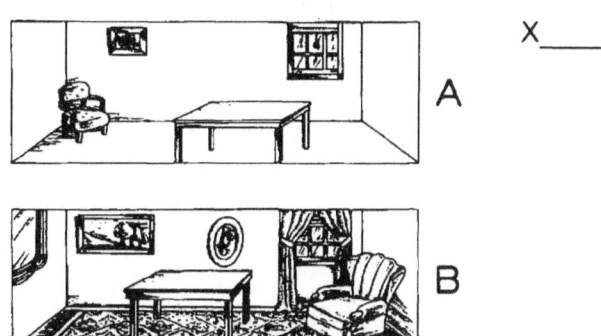

Y    Which would be the better shears for cutting metal?    Y____

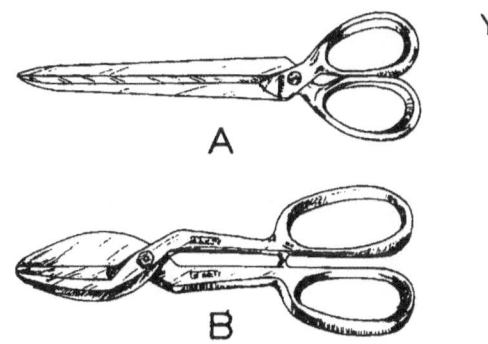

DIRECTIONS: Each question or incomplete statement is followed by two suggested answers or completions. Select A, B or C if the two figures have the same value, as the BEST answer that completes the statement or completes the statement.
*PRINT THE LETTER OF THE CORRECT ANSWER IN THE SPACE AT THE RIGHT.*

1.    Which airplane is turning to the right?    1.____

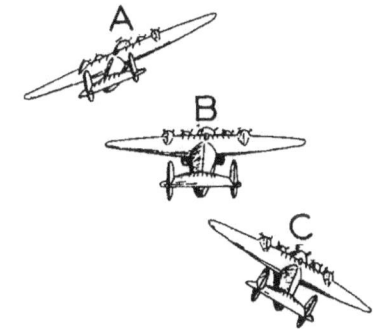

41

2. Which gear will make the most turns in a minute?   2.____

3. Which cart is more likely to tip over on the hillside?   3.____

4. Which wheel presses harder against the rail?   4.____

5. Which stepladder is safer to climb on?   5.____

6. Which spot on the wheel travels faster?   6.____

7. Which staircase would take less room?  7.____

8. Which man can lift more weight?  8.____

9. If the two men are pushing against the pushball in the directions shown, in which direction is it MOST likely to go?  9.____

10. Which of these objects is made of the heavier material?  10.____

11. Which man carries more weight?  11.____

12. Which wall will keep a house warmer in winter?  12.____

13. Which horse will be harder to hold?  13.____

14. Which man has to pull harder?  14.____

15. If the small wheel goes in the direction shown, in which direction will the large wheel go?  15.____

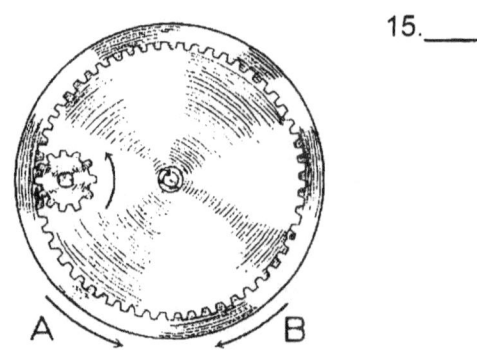

16. Which ounce of ice will cool a drink more quickly?

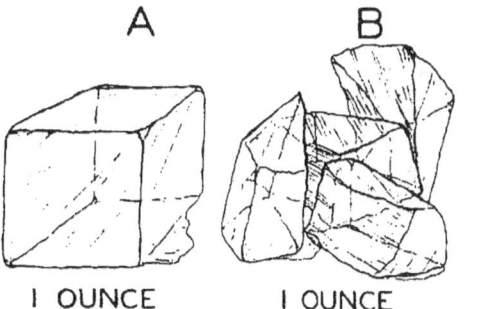

16.\_\_\_\_

17. If a can is heated, it is MOST likely to look like which one?

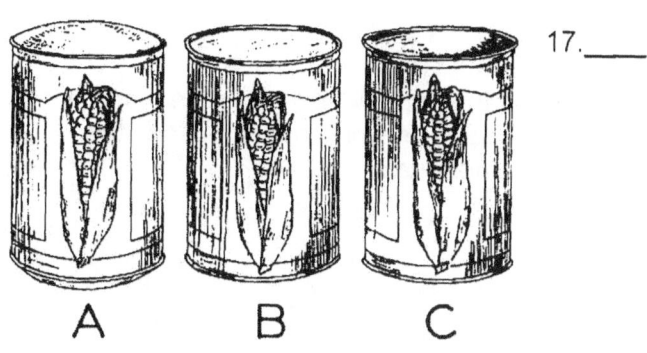

17.\_\_\_\_

18. Which rope is under more strain?

18.\_\_\_\_

19. Which gear will turn the same way as the driver?

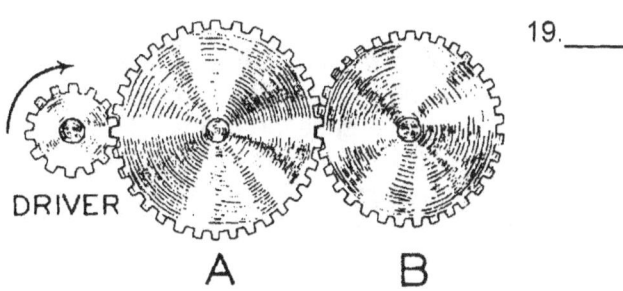

19.\_\_\_\_

20. If the two boys weigh the same, which of them can balance a heavier boy on the other end of his seesaw?

20.____

21. If the upper wheel moves in the direction shown, in which direction does the other one move?

21.____

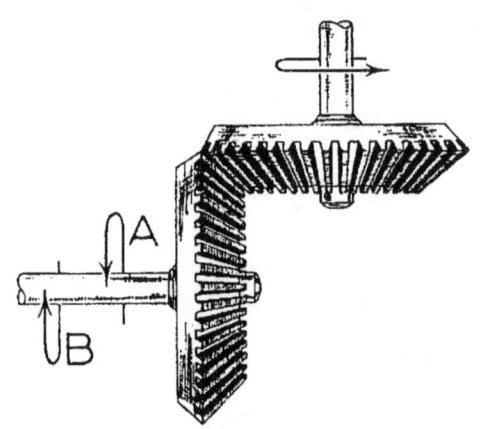

22. Which way will the boat go?

22.____

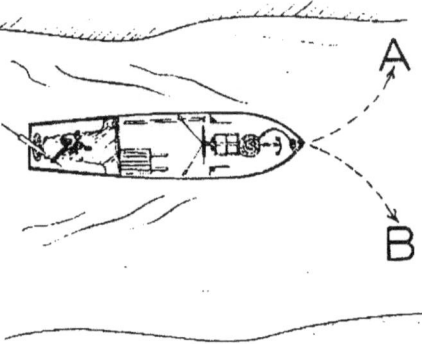

23. The man will hear the sound of the cannon:
    A. before he sees the flash
    B. after he sees the flash
    C. at the same time as he sees the flash

23.____

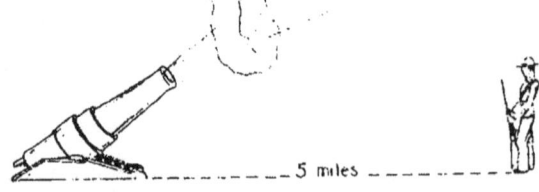

24. Which windmill will do more work?   24.\_\_\_\_

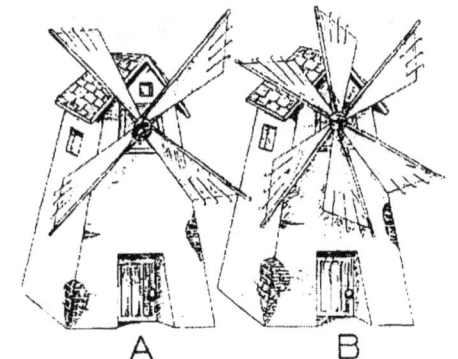

25. Which of these solid blocks will be the harder to tip over?   25.\_\_\_\_

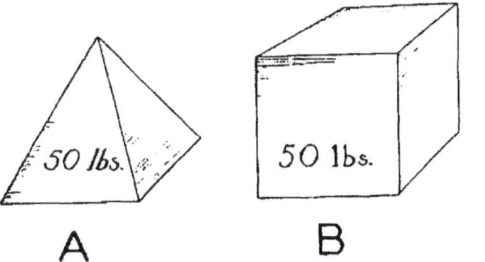

26. Which side of the road should be built higher?   26.\_\_\_\_

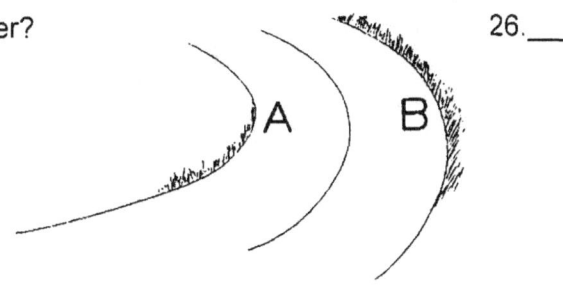

27. With which windlass can a man raise the heavier weight?   27.\_\_\_\_

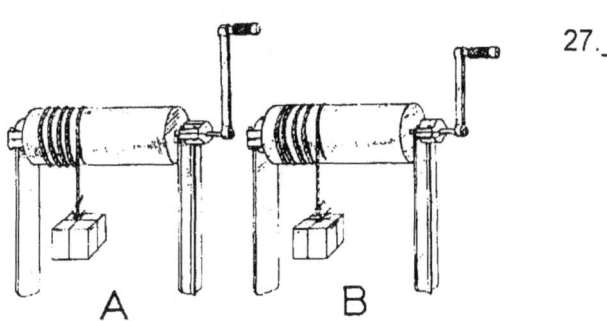

28. Which frying pan will be easier to handle?  28.____

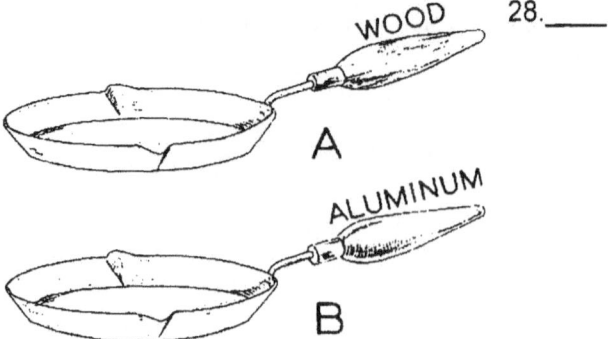

29. Which cow would be harder to see from an airplane?  29.____

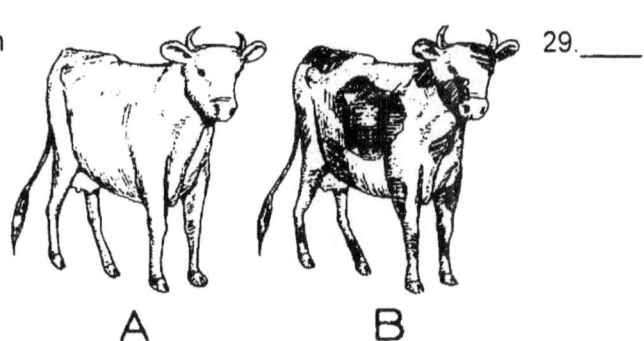

30. Which chain has more strain put upon it?  30.____

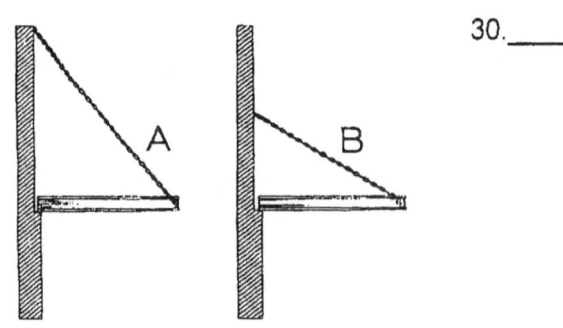

31. Which wheel will keep going longer after the power has been shut off?  31.____

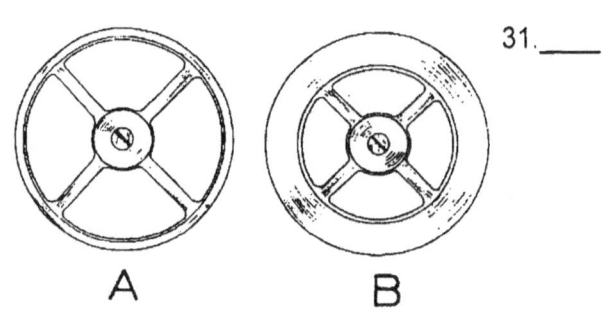

32. Which picture shows the way a bomb falls from a moving airplane if there is no wind?  32.____

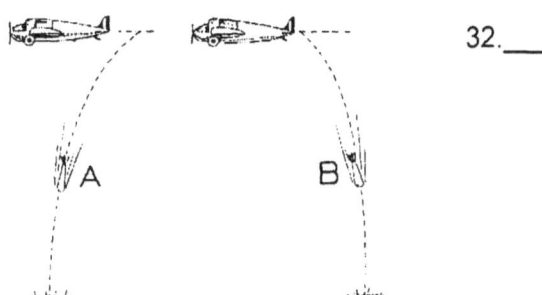

33. If the rock and tank of water together in Picture I weigh 100 pounds, they will weigh _____ in Picture II.
    A. more
    B. less
    C. the same

33.____

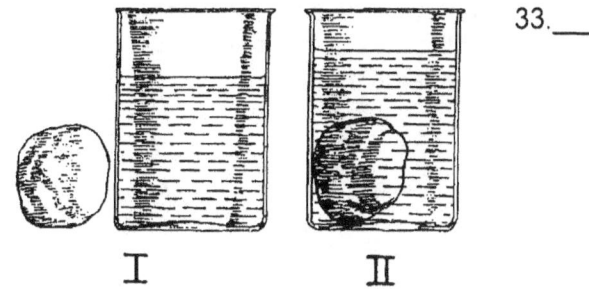

34. If light travels more slowly through glass than through air, which shape lens will make objects look larger?  34.____

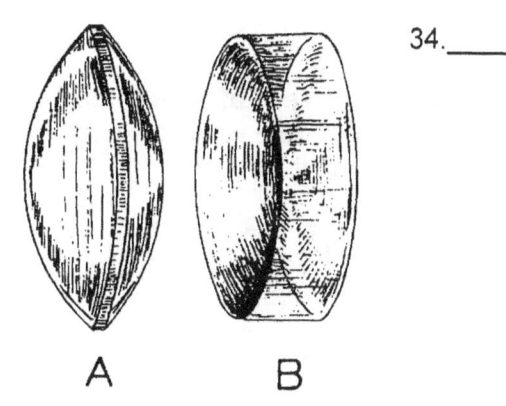

35. If a man were lifting a stone with this crowbar, at which point would the bar be MOST likely to break?  35.____

36. This wrench can be used to turn the pipe in which direction?  36._____

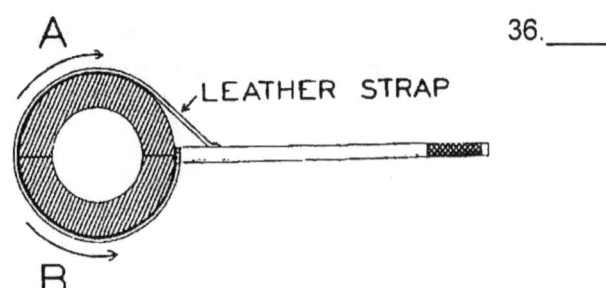

37. Which will use more current: the two bulbs at A, or the bulb at B? If the same, mark C.  37._____

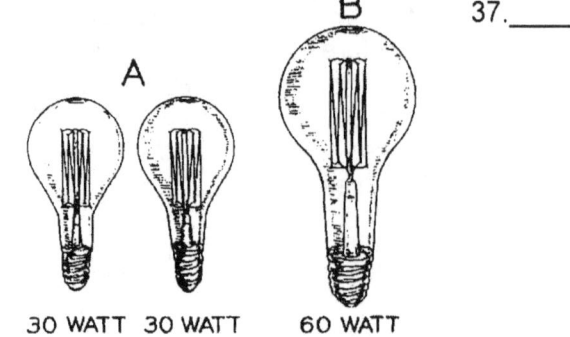

38. Which end of the toy horse will buck more when it is pulled along the floor?  38._____

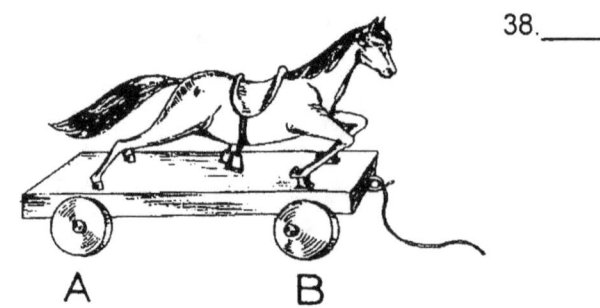

39. In which direction does the water in the right-hand pipe go?  39._____

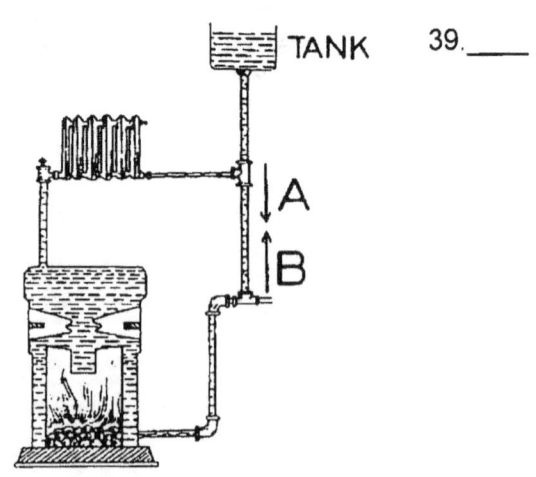

40. If the string shown by the arrow is plucked on the first harp, which string on the second harp will be more likely to sound?

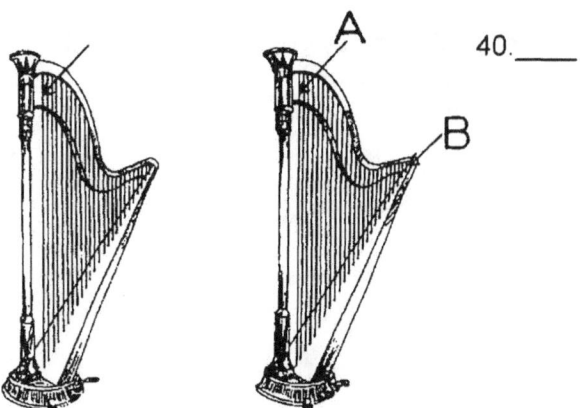

41. Which of these clocks will tick faster?

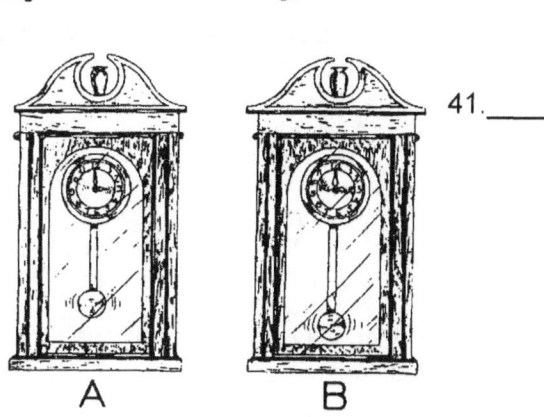

42. If the track is exactly level, on which rail does more pressure come?

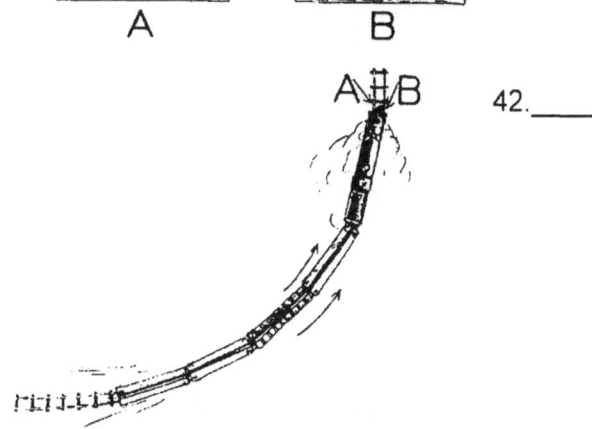

43. If there are no clouds, on which night will you be able to see more stars?

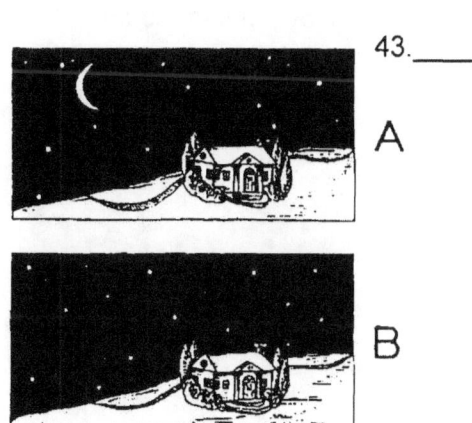

44. Which boy gets more light on the pages of his book?  44.\_\_\_\_

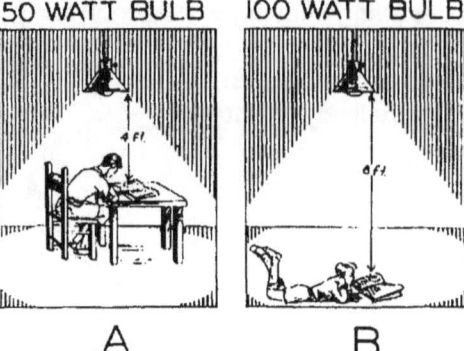

45. Which rock will get hotter in the sun?  45.\_\_\_\_

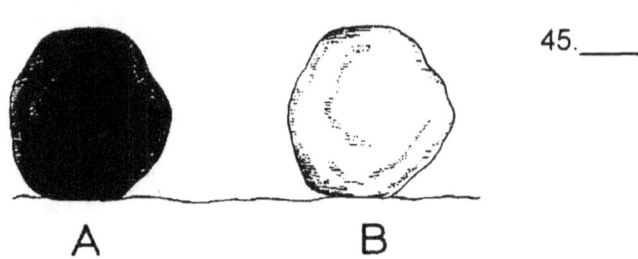

46. Which way can the man push the heavier load?  46.\_\_\_\_

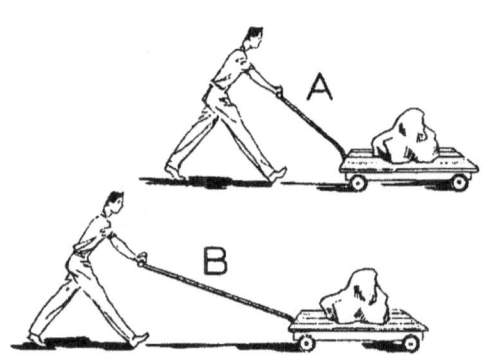

47. The top of the wheel "X" will go:  47.\_\_\_\_
    A. steadily to the right
    B. steadily to the left
    C. by jerks to the left

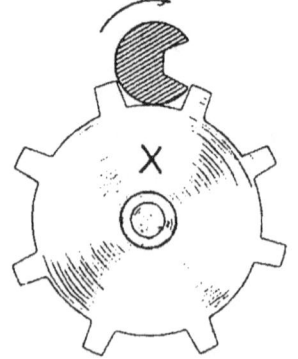

48. Which wire carries more current?   48.____

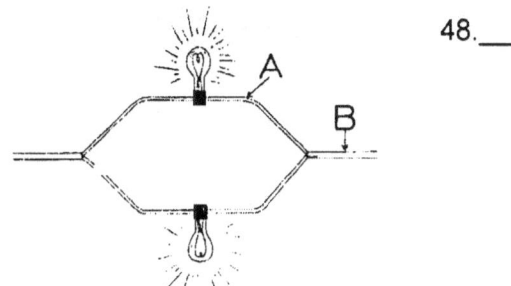

49. Which tank will empty faster?   49.____

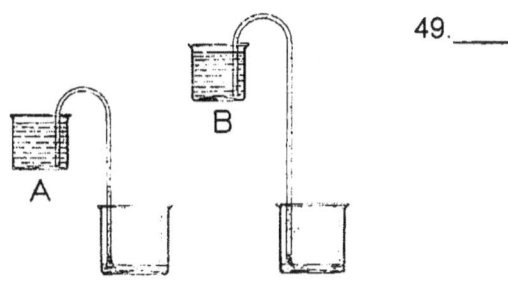

50. At which point will the boat be lower in the water?   50.____

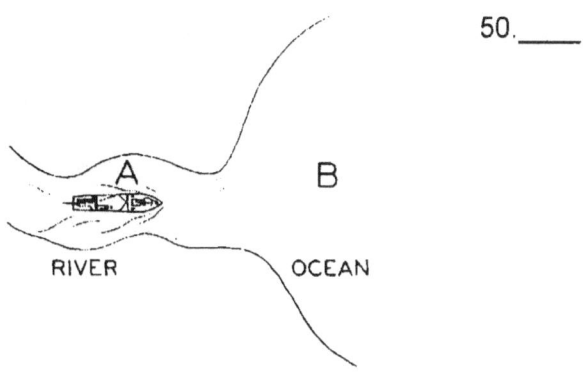

51. To pull this boat along the canal, at which point is it better to attach the rope?   51.____

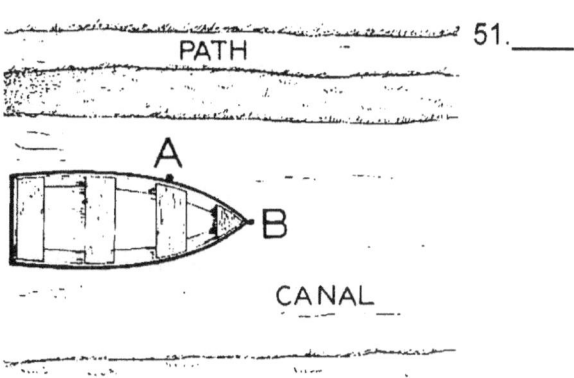

52. Which weighs more?

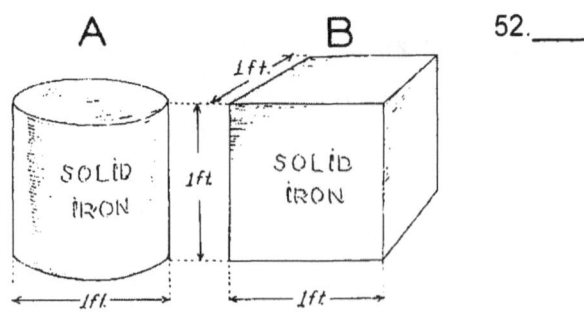

53. When the little wheel turns around, the big wheel will:
    A. turn in direction A
    B. turn in direction B
    C. move back and forth

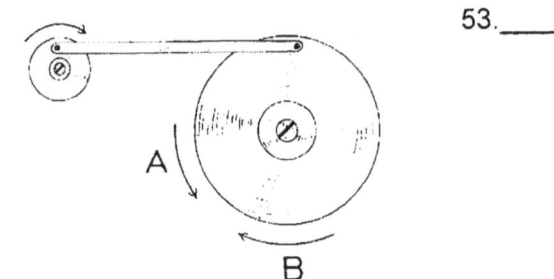

54. Which arrow shows the way the air will move along the floor when the radiator is turned on?

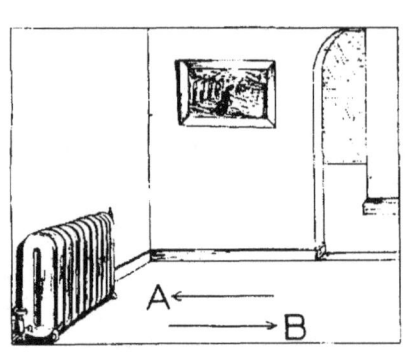

55. Which weighs more?

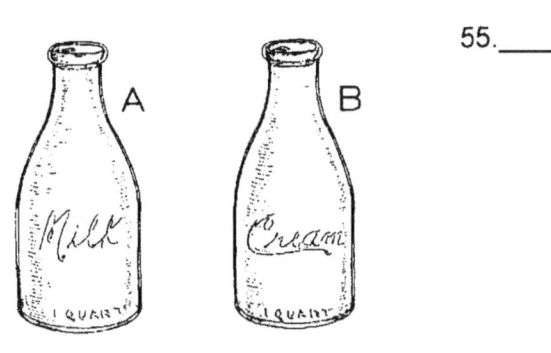

56. Which of these is the more likely picture of a train wreck?

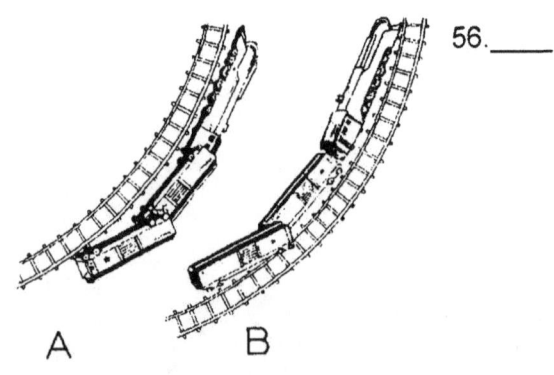

52.____

53.____

54.____

55.____

56.____

57. Which of these wires offers more resistance to the passage of an electric current?

57.____

58. Which spot on the wheel travels faster?

58.____

59. Which cannon will shoot farthest?

59.____

60. With which arrangement can a man lift the heavier weight?

60.____

## KEY (CORRECT ANSWERS)

| | | | | | |
|---|---|---|---|---|---|
| 1. C | 11. B | 21. A | 31. B | 41. A | 51. B |
| 2. C | 12. B | 22. A | 32. A | 42. B | 52. B |
| 3. A | 13. A | 23. B | 33. C | 43. B | 53. C |
| 4. B | 14. B | 24. B | 34. A | 44. A | 54. A |
| 5. A | 15. A | 25. A | 35. A | 45. A | 55. B |
| 6. C | 16. B | 26. B | 36. A | 46. A | 56. A |
| 7. B | 17. A | 27. A | 37. C | 47. C | 57. A |
| 8. B | 18. A | 28. A | 38. B | 48. B | 58. B |
| 9. B | 19. B | 29. B | 39. A | 49. B | 59. B |
| 10. B | 20. B | 30. B | 40. A | 50. A | 60. B |

# MECHANICAL APTITUDE

# MECHANICAL REASONING
## DIRECTIONS

This test consists of a number of pictures and questions about those pictures. Look at Example X on this page to see just what to do. Example X shows a picture of two men carrying a machine part on a board and asks, "Which man has the heavier load? If equal, mark C." Man "B" has the heavier load because the weight is closer to him than to man "A," so on the separate Answer Sheet you would fill in the space under B, like this

Now look at Example Y. The question asks, "Which weighs more? If equal, mark C." As the scale is perfectly balanced, "A" and "B" must weigh the same, so you would blacken the space under C on your separate Answer Sheet, like this

---

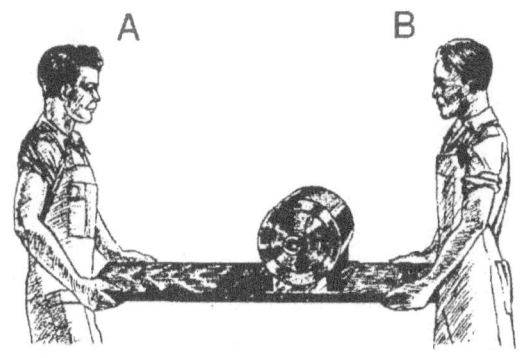

X

Which man has the heavier load?
(If equal, mark C.)

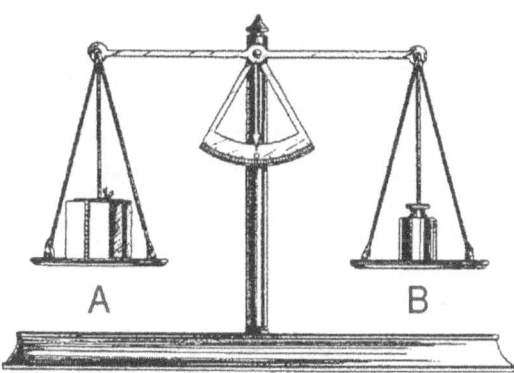

Y

Which weighs more?
(If equal, mark C.)

---

On the following pages there are more pictures and questions. Read each question carefully, look at the picture, and mark your answer on the separate Answer Sheet. Do not forget that there is a third choice for every question.

**1**

When these soldiers march around the corner, which man goes further?
(If equal, mark C.)

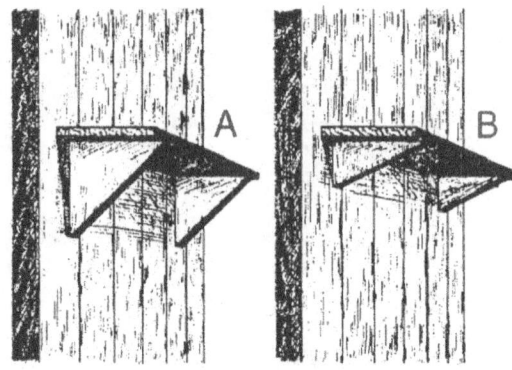

**2**

Which shelf is stronger?
(If equal, mark C.)

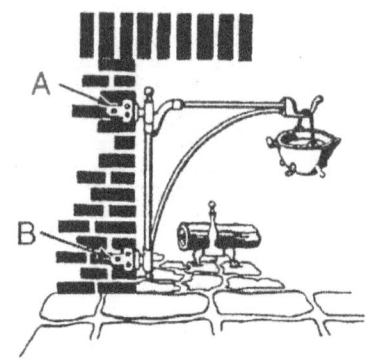

**3**

Which hinge is more likely to pull out of the brick wall?
(If equal, mark C.)

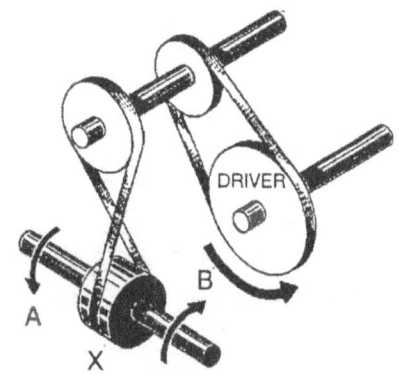

**4**

If the driver turns in the direction shown, which way will the pulley at "X" turn?
(If either, mark C.)

3 (#1)

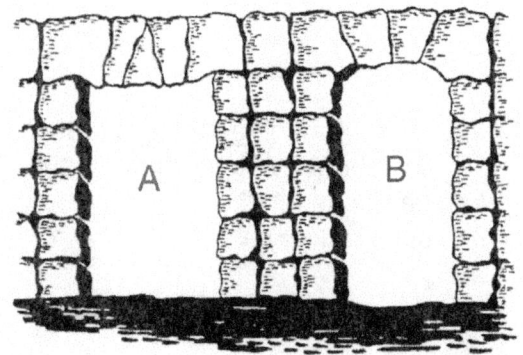

**5**

Which archway is stronger?
(If equal, mark C.)

**6**

In which picture can the ferry cross the river more quickly?
(If either, mark C.)

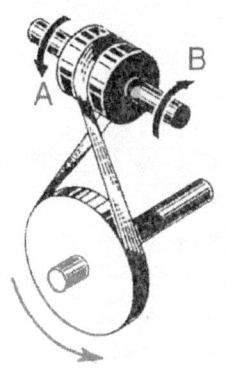

**7**

When the bottom pulley turns in the direction shown, which way does the top pulley turn?
(If either, mark C.)

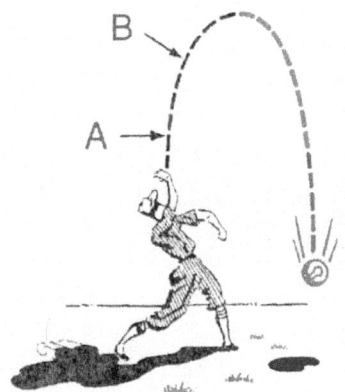

**8**

At which point was the ball going faster?
(If equal, mark C.)

4 (#1)

**9**

When the left-hand gear turns in the direction shown, which way does the right-hand one turn?
(If either, mark C.)

**10**

Which tread must stop for the tank to turn in the direction shown?
(If neither, mark C.)

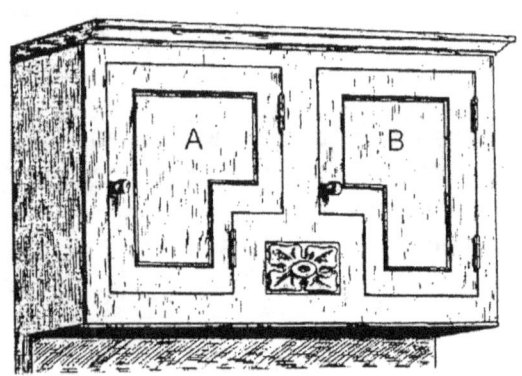

**11**

Which door will swing better on its hinges?
(If neither, mark C.)

**12**

When the bicycle wheel stops moving, which arrow shows where the tire valve will stop?

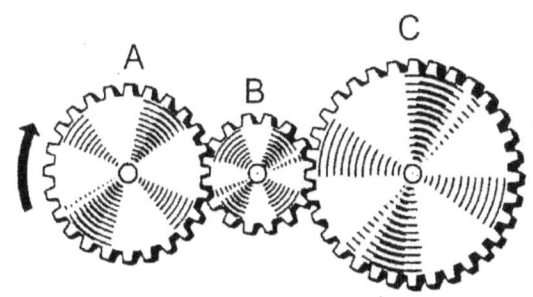

**13**

Which gear turns the least number of times in a minute?

**14**

Which picture shows the easier way for the men to lift the pipe?
(If equal, mark C.)

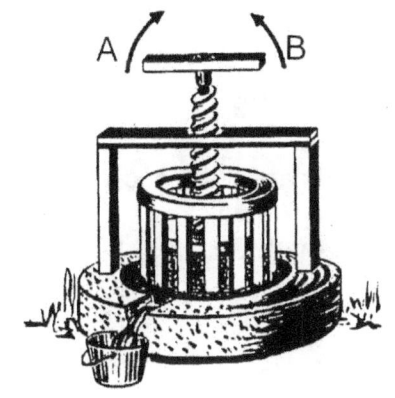

**15**

Which way should the handle be turned to press juice from fruit?
(If either, mark C.)

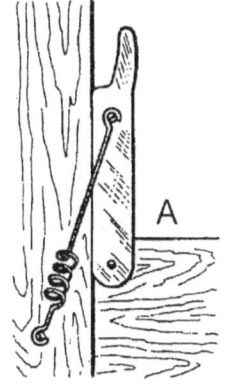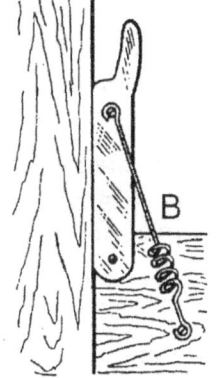

**16**

In which picture will the spring hold the handle where it now is?
(If both, mark C.)

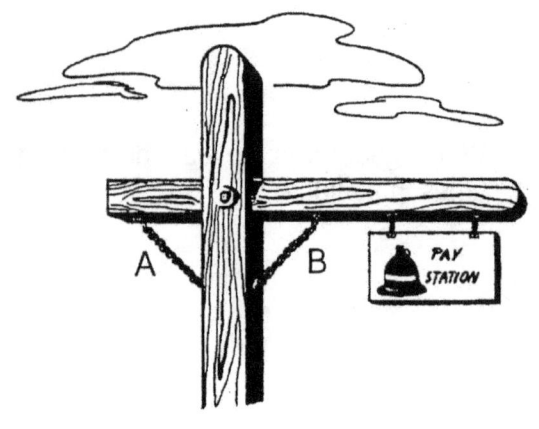

**17**

Which chain alone will hold up the sign?
(If either, mark C.)

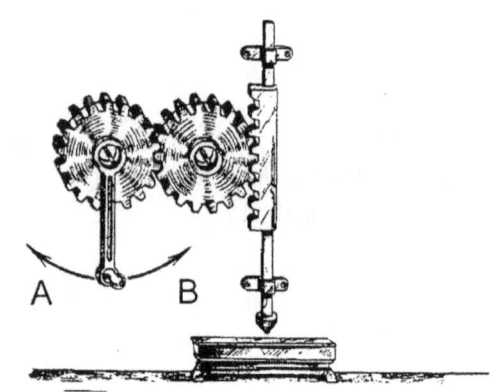

**18**

Which way should the handle be moved to push the point against the plate?
(If either, mark C.)

**19**

Which girl can lift the bucket of water more easily?
(If equal, mark C.)

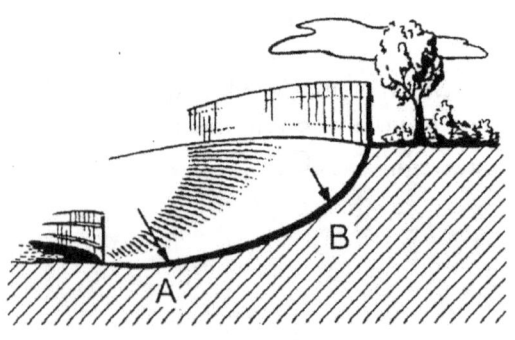

**20**

On which part of this race track will a very fast car make the turn?
(If either, mark C.)

7 (#1)

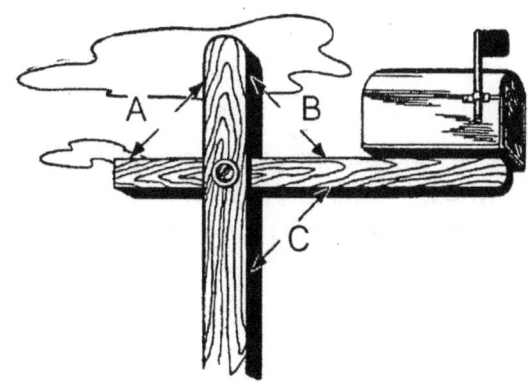

**21**

Which letter shows the best place for a chain support?

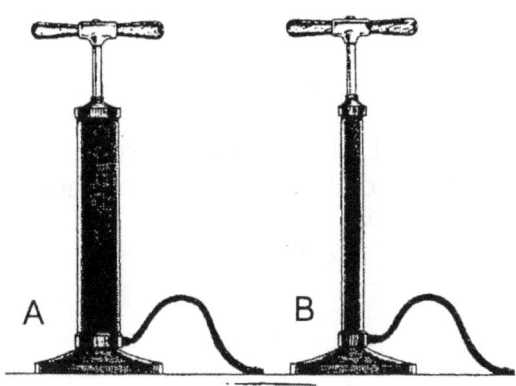

**22**

With which pump can you blow up a tube for swimming more quickly? (If either, mark C.)

**23**

Which wheel will turn more slowly? (If equal, mark C.)

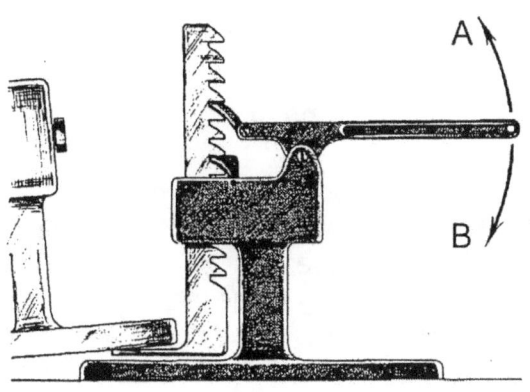

**24**

This jack lifts when the handle is moved in:
- (A) direction A;
- (B) direction B;
- (C) either direction.

8 (#1)

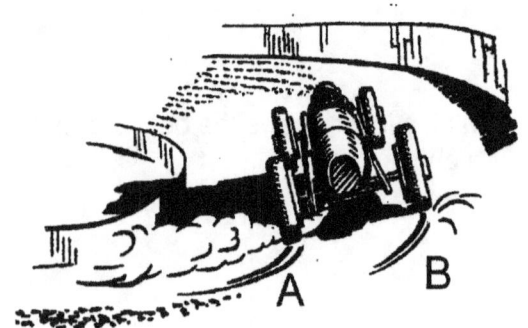

**25**

In racing around this track, which wheel travels further?
(If equal, mark C.)

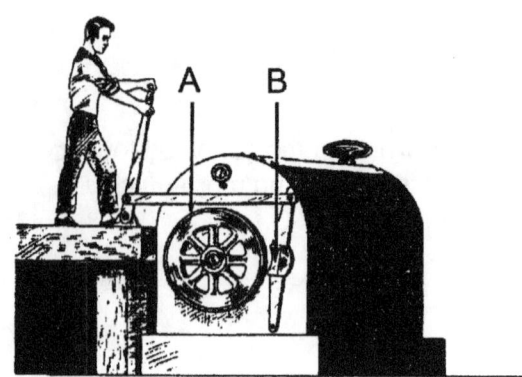

**26**

Which part will wear out more quickly if both the brake and wheel are made of iron?
(If equal, mark C.)

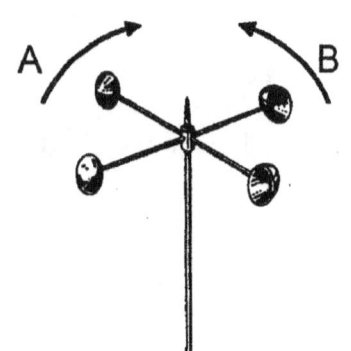

**27**

When the wind blows, in which direction will these cups turn?
(If either, mark C.)

**28**

When the upper wheel turns in the direction shown, the top of the lower wheel will move:
    (A)  steadily to the left;
    (B)  by jerks to the right;
    (C)  by jerks to the left.

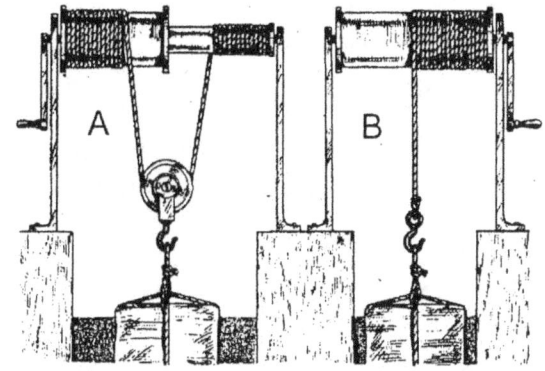

**29**

With which windlass can the heavier weight be lifted?
(If equal, mark C.)

**30**

Which picture shows the path of a thrown ball?
(If either, mark C.)

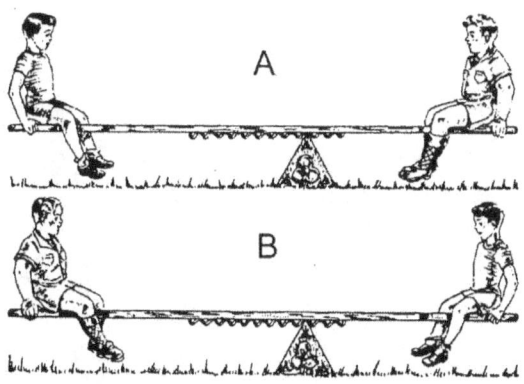

**31**

Which picture shows how the two boys will balance better?
(If equal, markC.)

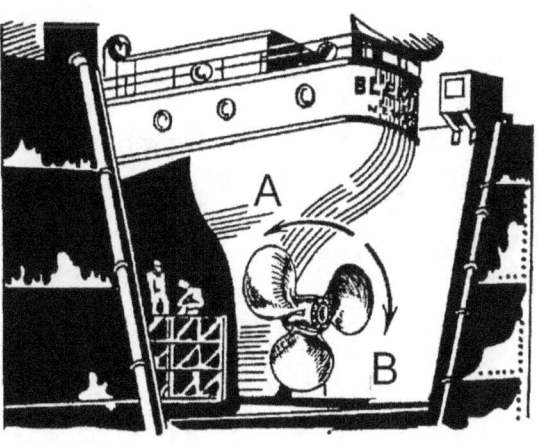

**32**

In which direction must the propeller turn to drive the ship forward?
(If either, mark C.)

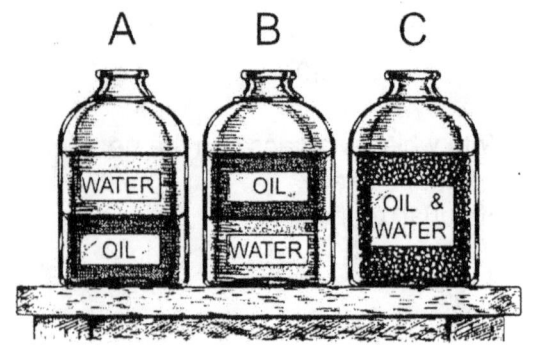

33

Which picture shows how oil and water would be after standing for a while?

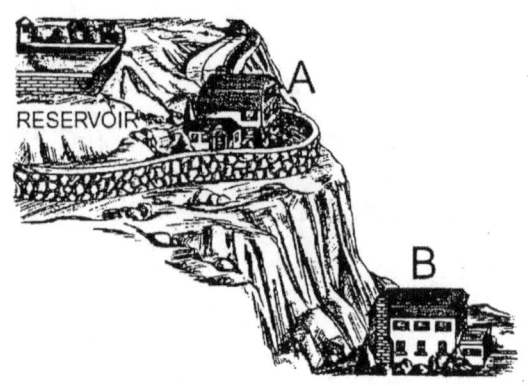

34

At which house will a hose throw water further?
(If either, mark C.)

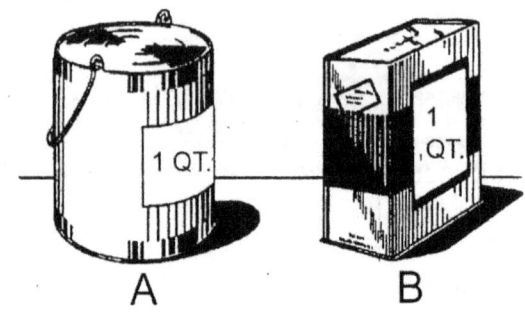

35

Which shape can will need the bigger carton for a dozen quarts?
(If equal, mark C.)

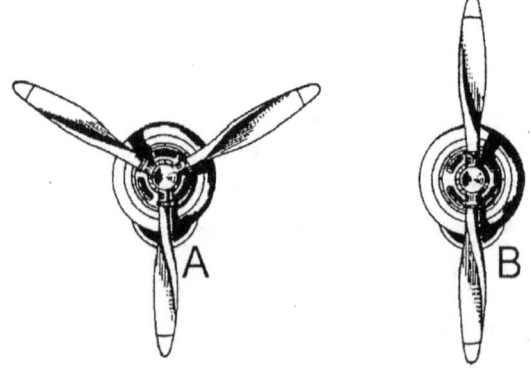

36

Which propeller needs the more powerful engine to turn it at a given speed?
(If equal, mark C.)

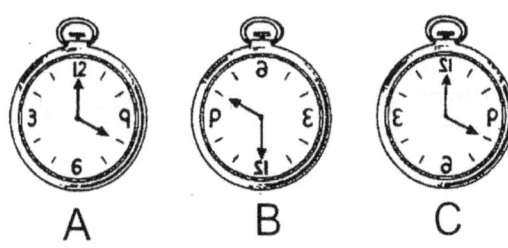

**37**

Which picture shows how a clock looks when seen in a mirror?

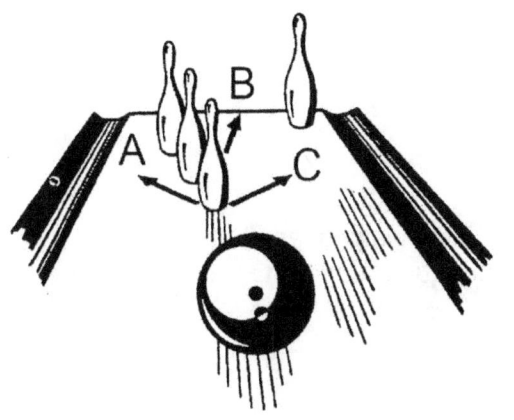

**38**

Which way will the pin go after the bowling ball hits it?

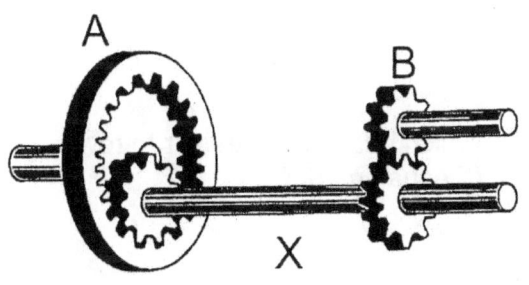

**39**

Which gear turns the same way as shaft "X"?
(If both, mark C.)

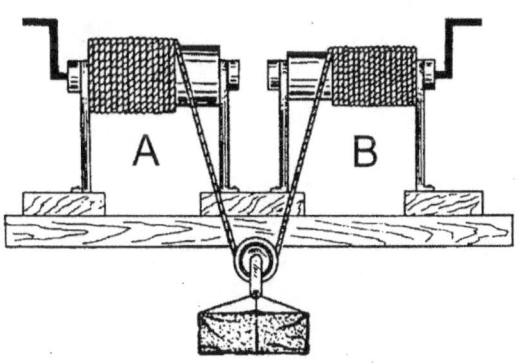

**40**

Which windlass must be turned more times to lift the weight five feet?
(If equal, mark C.)

12 (#1)

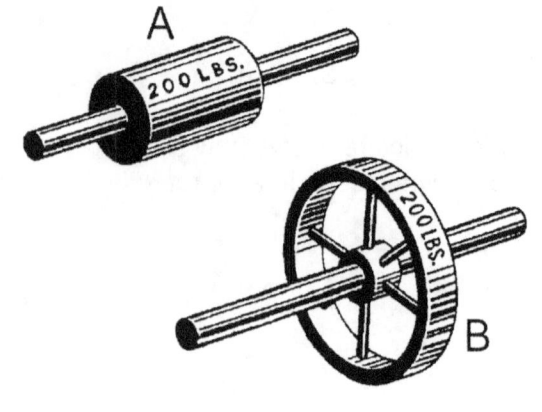

41

Which flywheel will keep its shaft turning longer?
(If equal, mark C.)

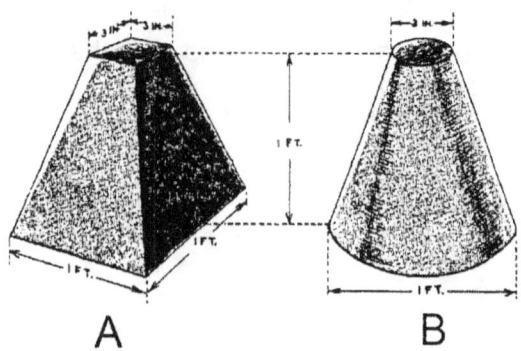

42

Which weighs less?
(If equal, mark C.)

43

Which boat will be easier to row?
(If equal, mark C.)

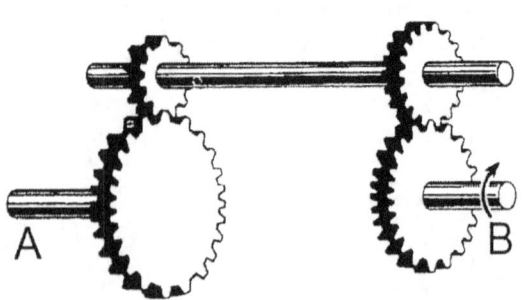

44

Which shaft will turn faster?
(If equal, mark C.)

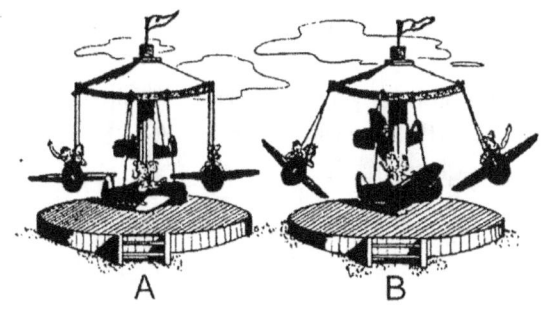

**45**

In which picture are the children pressed more firmly against the seats?
(If equal, mark C.)

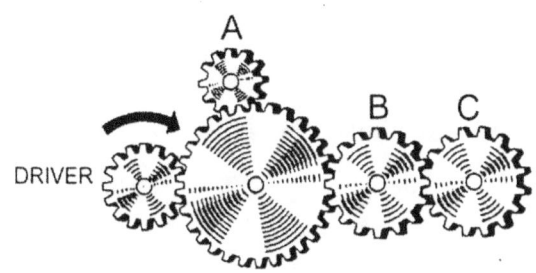

**46**

Which gear turns opposite to the driver?

 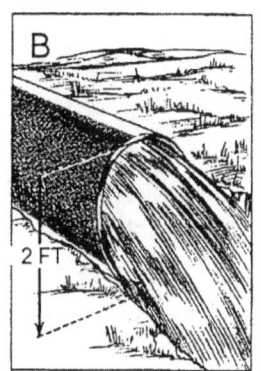

**47**

Which will carry more water, the two pipes in A or the one pipe in B?
(If equal, mark C.)

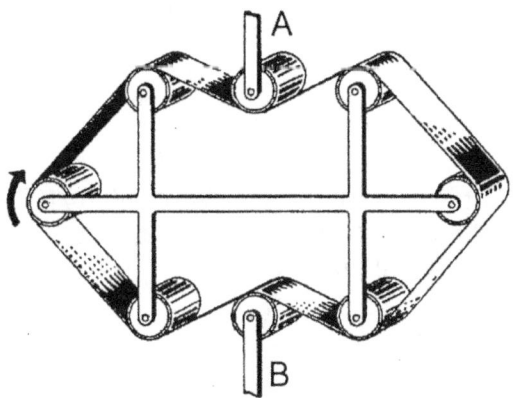

**48**

Which roller turns in the direction opposite to "X"?
(If both, mark C.)

14 (#1)

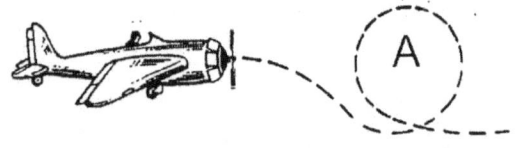
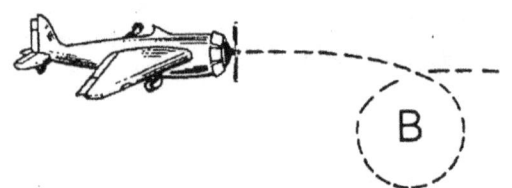

49

In which loop is the pilot more likely to fall out of the plane?
(If equal, mark C.)

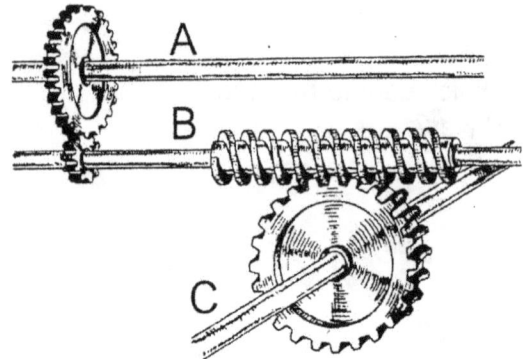

50

Which shaft can not be the driver?

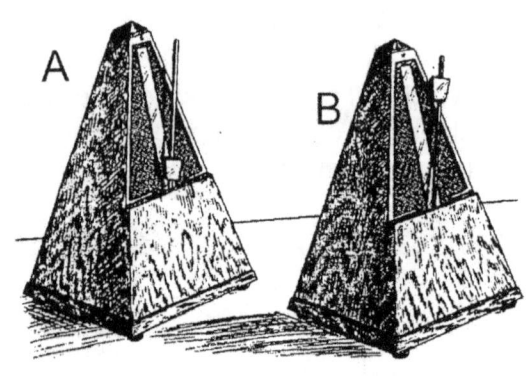

51

In which picture will the timer tick more slowly?
(If neither, mark C.)

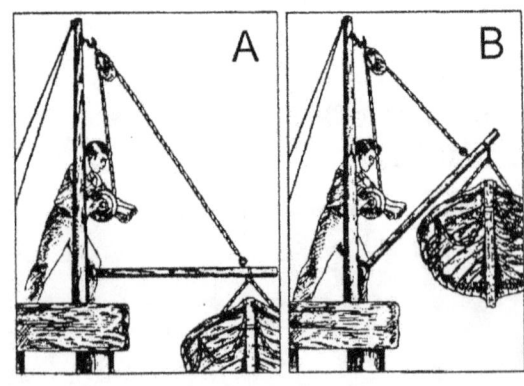

52

In which picture is it easier for the man to turn the crank?
(If equal, mark C.)

15 (#1)

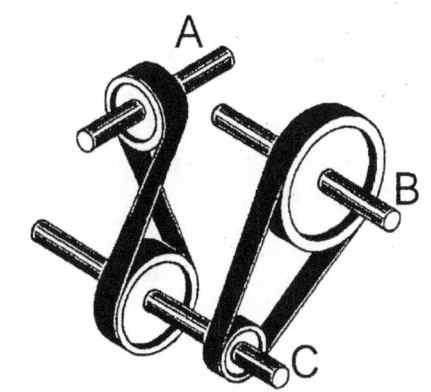

**53**

Which shaft will turn most slowly?

**54**

Which boy is pushing harder?
(If equal, mark C.)

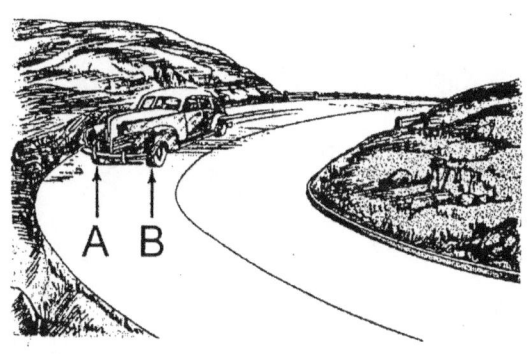

**55**

As this car goes around the turn, which tire presses harder on the road?
(If equal, mark C.)

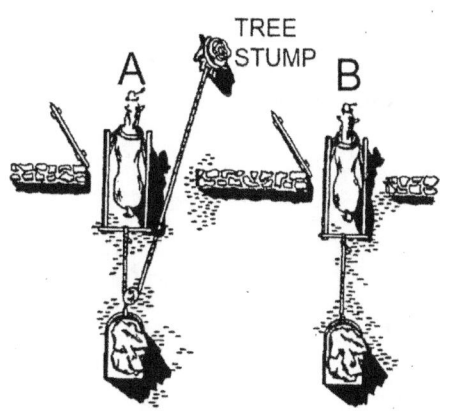

**56**

Which horse must walk further to pull the stone boat through the gate?
(If equal, mark C.)

16 (#1)

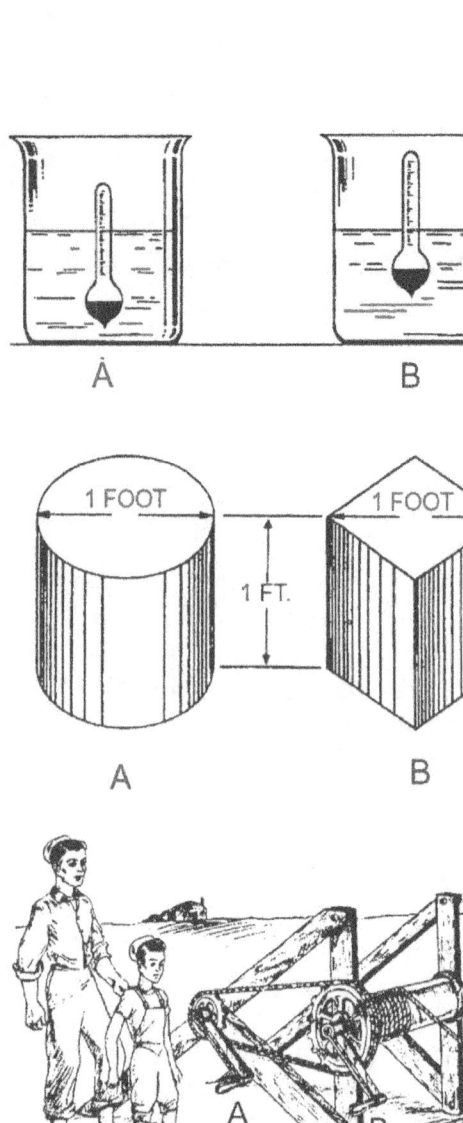

57

In which jar is the liquid lighter?
(If equal, mark C.)

58

Which weighs more?
(If equal, mark C.)

59

Which handle is better for the boy to turn?
(If either, mark C.)

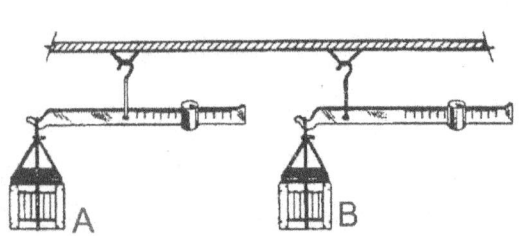

60

Which box weighs more?
(If equal, mark C.)

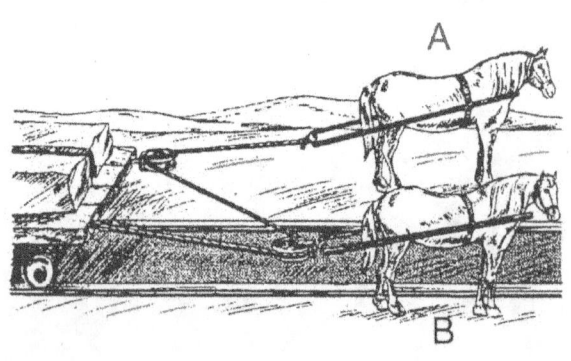

61

Which horse has to pull harder?
(If equal, mark C.)

17 (#1)

**62**

In which picture can the two men lift the anchor more easily?
(If equal, mark C.)

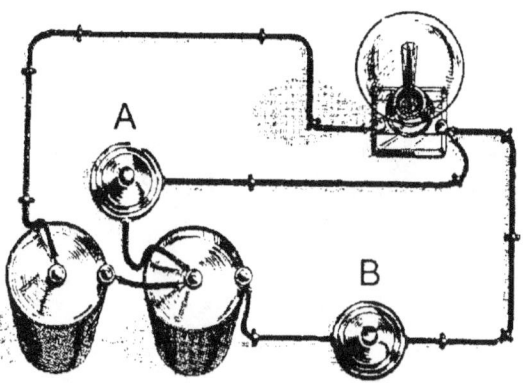

**63**

Which push button will make the bulb light more brightly?
(If equal, mark C.)

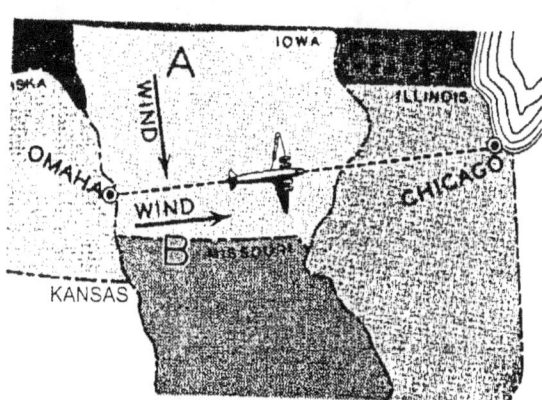

**64**

An airplane can make the round trip more quickly when the wind is in direction:
    (A) of arrow A;
    (B) of arrow B;
    (C) when there is no wind.

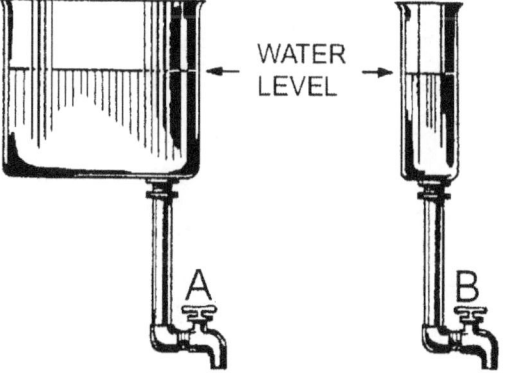

**65**

At which faucet is the water pressure greater? (If equal, mark C.)

18 (#1)

66

Which man has to pull harder?
(If equal, mark C.)

67

With which mirror can the driver see more of what is behind him?
(If equal, mark C.)

 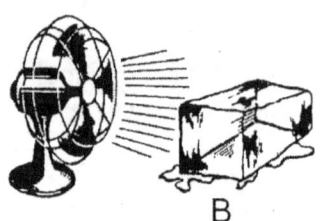

68

Which cake of ice will melt more quickly?
(If equal, mark C.)

19 (#1)

# KEY (CORRECT ANSWERS)

| | | | | |
|---|---|---|---|---|
| 1. B | 16. A | 31. A | 46. C | 61. B |
| 2. A | 17. A | 32. B | 47. B | 62. B |
| 3. A | 18. B | 33. B | 48. C | 63. A |
| 4. B | 19. B | 34. B | 49. B | 64. C |
| 5. B | 20. B | 35. A | 50. C | 65. A |
| 6. B | 21. B | 36. A | 51. B | 66. A |
| 7. B | 22. A | 37. C | 52. B | 67. A |
| 8. A | 23. A | 38. A | 53. B | 68. A |
| 9. B | 24. B | 39. A | 54. A | |
| 10. B | 25. B | 40. B | 55. A | |
| 11. B | 26. B | 41. B | 56. A | |
| 12. C | 27. B | 42. B | 57. A | |
| 13. C | 28. C | 43. B | 58. A | |
| 14. A | 29. A | 44. B | 59. A | |
| 15. A | 30. A | 45. B | 60. B | |

# MECHANICAL APTITUDE
## TEST OF
## MECHANICAL COMPREHENSION

### DIRECTIONS

Fill in the requested information on your ANSWER SHEET.

Then look at Sample X on this page. It shows two tables loaded with dishes and asks, "Which table is more likely to break?" Table "B" is more likely to break because the heaviest weight is located at the edge of the table where the support is weakest; so blacken the space under "B" on your answer sheet. Now look at Sample Y and answer it yourself. Fill in the space under the correct answer on your answer sheet.

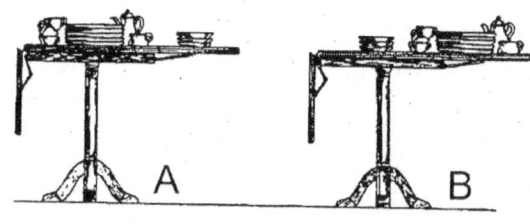

X

Which table is more likely to break?

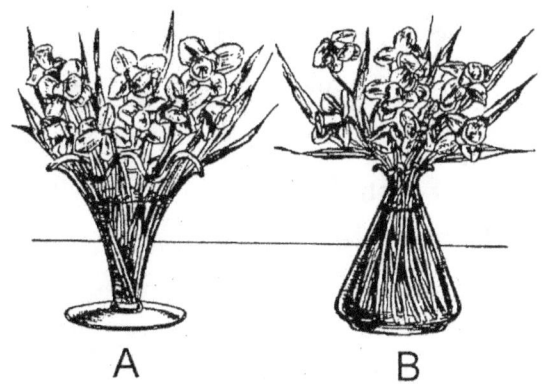

Y

Which vase of flowers will tip over more easily?

On the following pages there are more pictures and questions. Read each question carefully, look at the picture, and fill in the space under the best answer on the answer sheet. Make sure that your marks are heavy and black. Erase completely any answer you wish to change.

2 (#1)

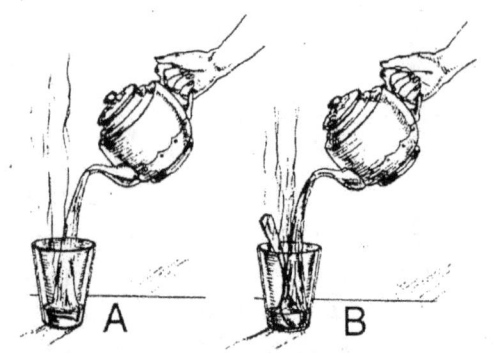

1.

Which glass is more likely to break?

2.

Which is the better way to take a wheelbarrow over the curb?

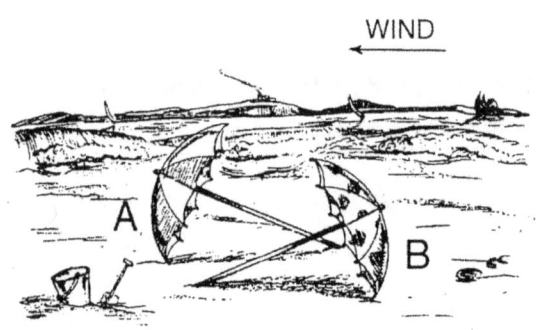

3.

Which beach umbrella is more likely to blow away?

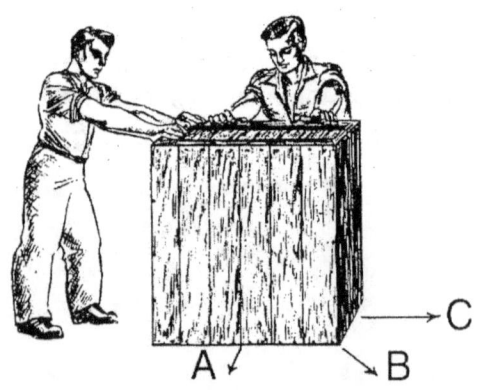

4.

In which direction will the crate go if the men push against it with equal force?

3 (#1)

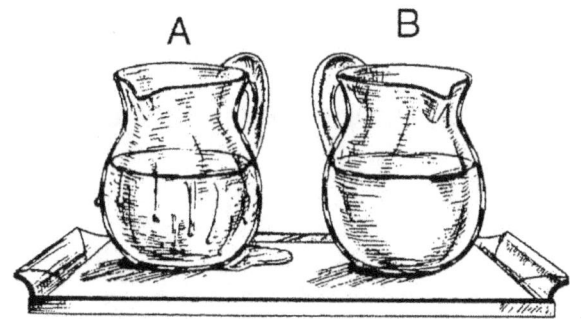

5. In which pitcher is the water colder?

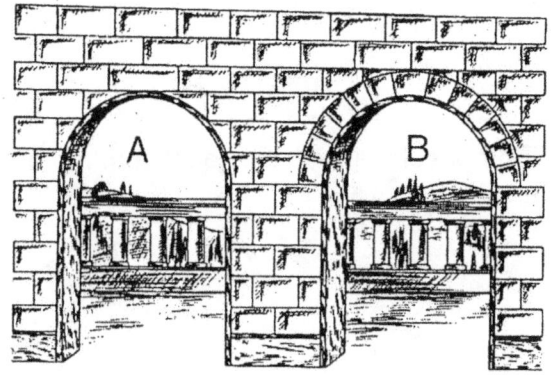

6. Which arch is stronger?

7. Which is the better way to ventilate the kitchen?

8. With which spoon will it be easier to stir the boiling syrup?

4 (#1)

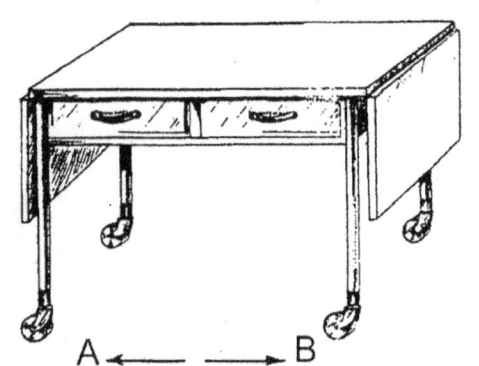

9.

In which direction was the table rolling?

10.

From which can will the liquid pour more easily?

A
(Large pupil)

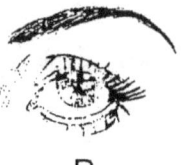
B
(Small pupil)

11.

Which way will an eye appear in the dark?

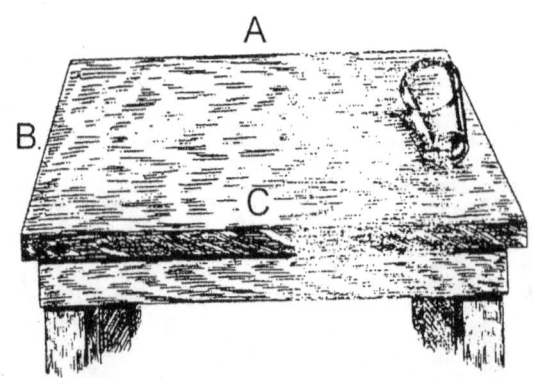

12.

Off which edge of the table will the glass roll?

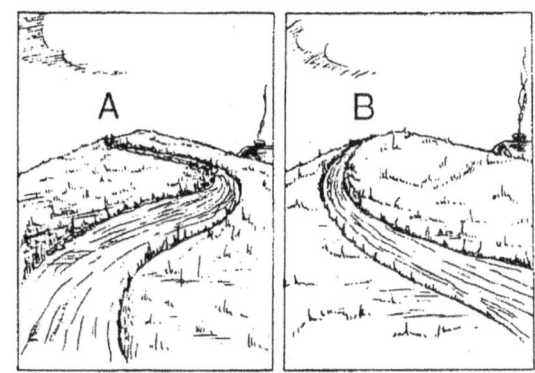

13.

Which path is steeper?

14.

Which wheel turns around more times in going a block?

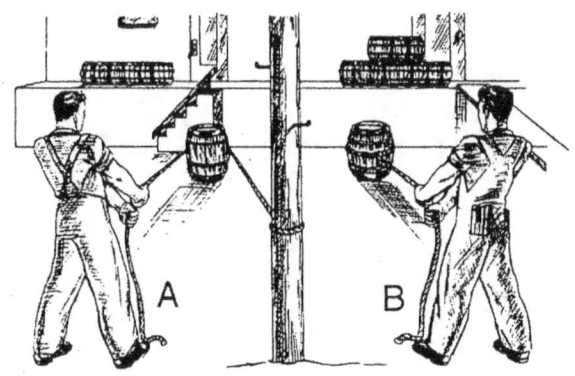

15.

Which man has to pull harder to move the barrel?

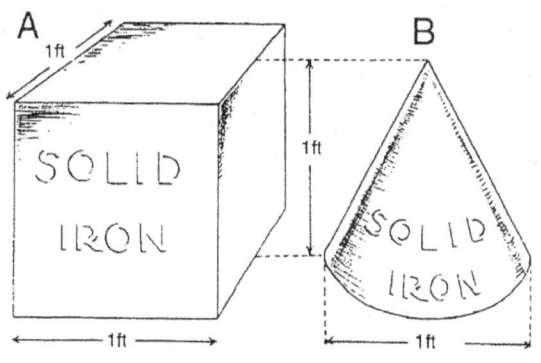

16.

Which weighs more?

6 (#1)

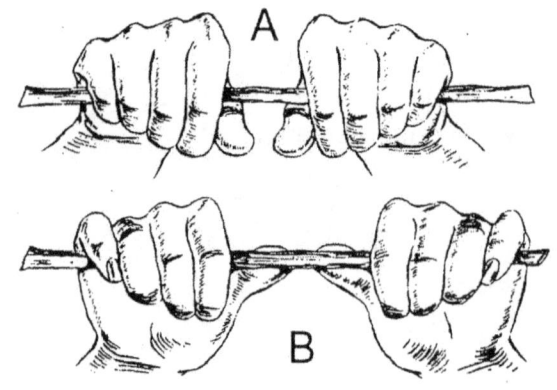

17.

Which is the better way to break the twig?

18.

Which cup of coffee will cool more rapidly?

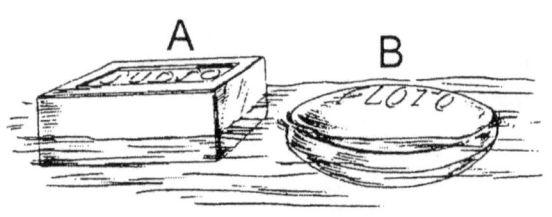

19.

Which is made of the heavier material?

20.

Which is the better way to lift the shovel?

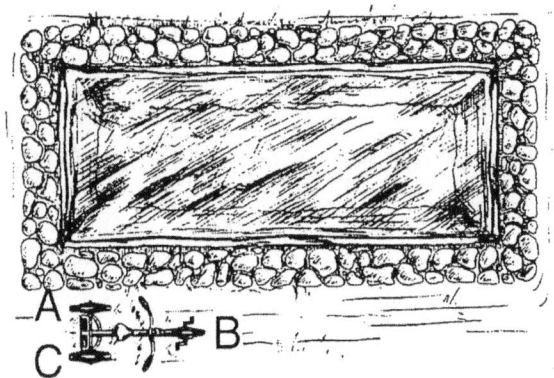

21.

Which wheel of the tricycle goes farthest when it is ridden around the pool?

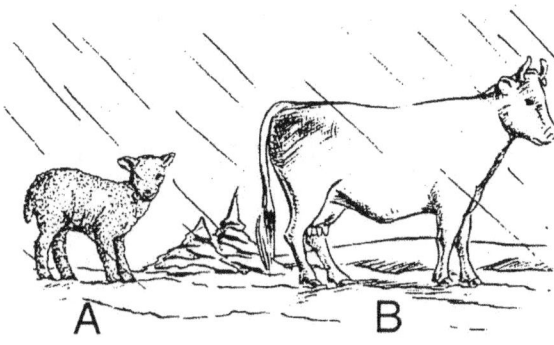

22.

On which animal's back will the snow melt more rapidly?

23.

Which girl can swing back and forth more times in a minute?

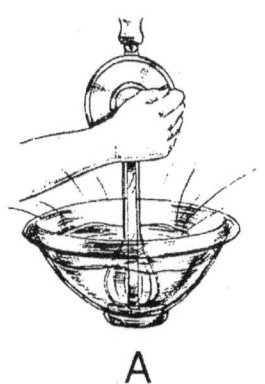 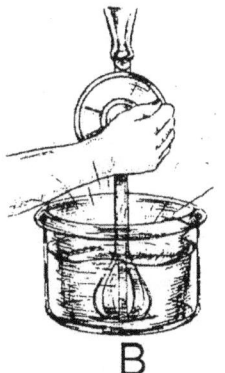

24.

From which bowl will the liquid splash more?

8 (#1)

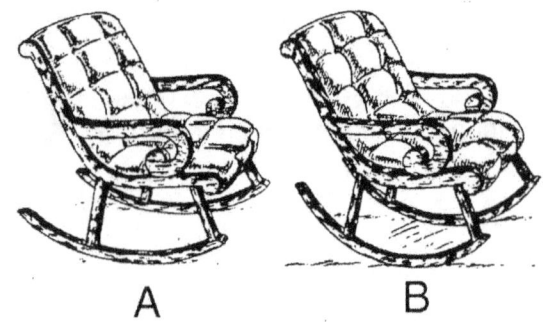

25.

Which rocking chair will tip over more easily?

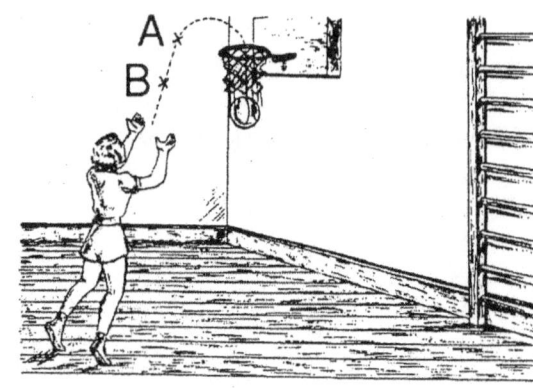

26.

At which point was the ball going faster?

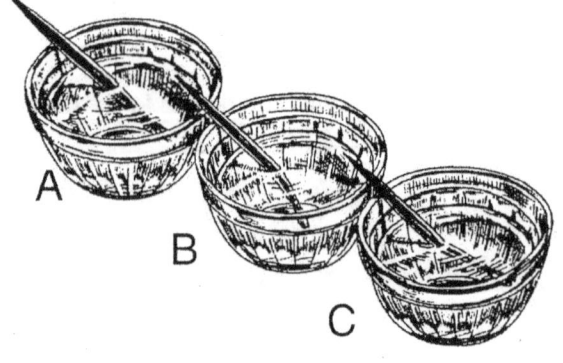

27.

Which picture shows the way a paint brush would look in a bowl of water?

28.

Which girl is more likely to trip?

9 (#1)

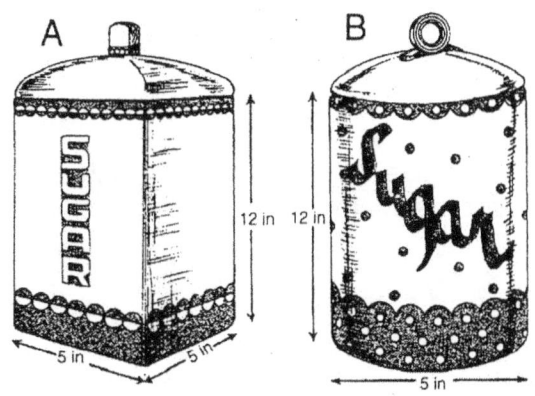

29.

Which metal con'tainer will hold more sugar?

30.

Which coat will sink farther into the snow if the sun is shining?

31.

In which direction is the truck more likely to go off the road?

32.

Which end of the cord should you pull to open the curtain?

10 (#1)

33.

If the ropes are very weak, in which case is the man safer?

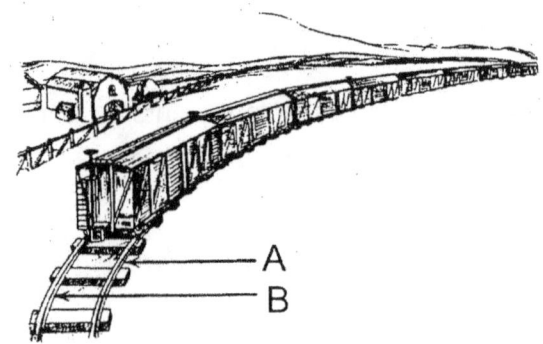

34.

Which rail should be built higher?

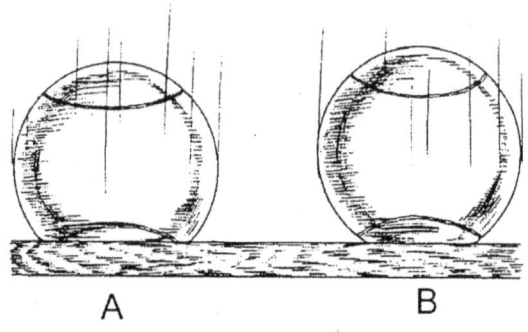

35.

If the two tennis balls have been dropped from the same height, which one will bounce higher?

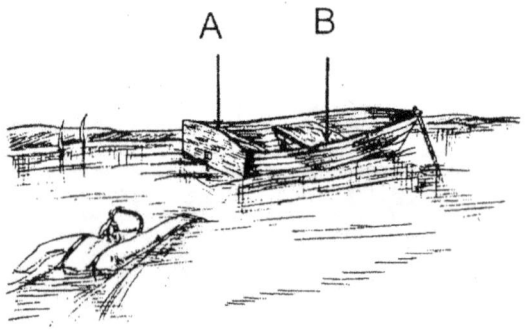

36.

At which point is it better for the girl to climb into the boat?

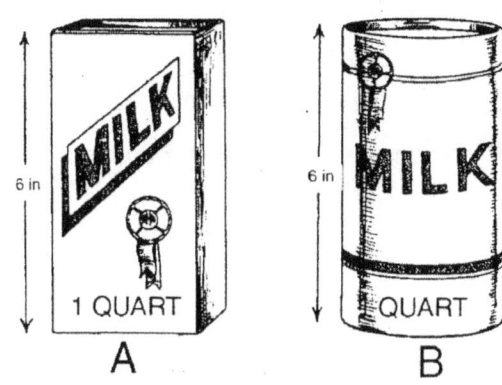

37.

Which shape milk container would use less cardboard?

38.

Which clown will jump more when the toy is pulled?

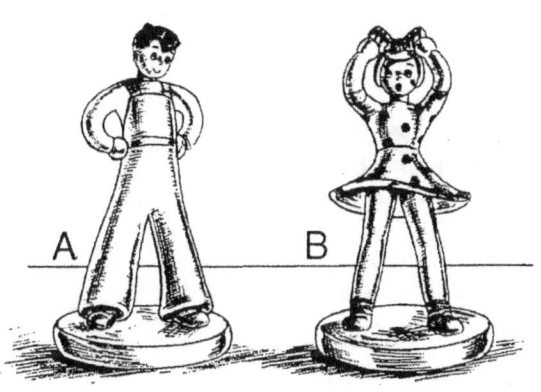

39.

Which statuette will tip over more easily?

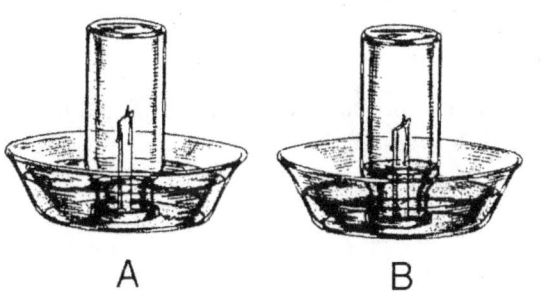

40.

In which picture has the candle been burning?

12 (#1)

41.

Which gate will close better by itself?

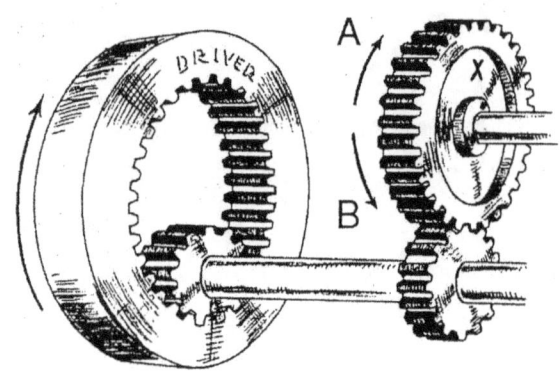

42.

If the driver turns in the direction shown, in which direction will gear "X" move?

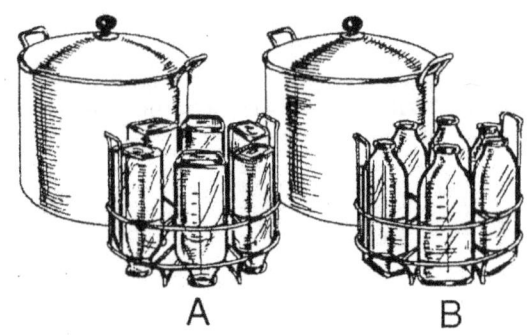

43.

Which is the better way to place the bottles in the rack to sterilize them?

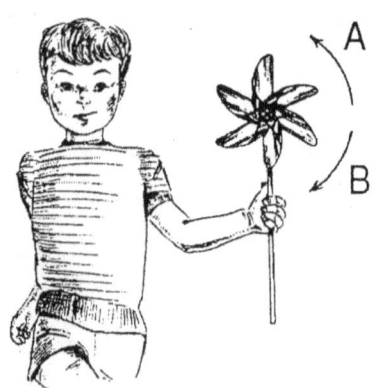

44.

In which direction will the pin-wheel turn as the boy runs?

13 (#1)

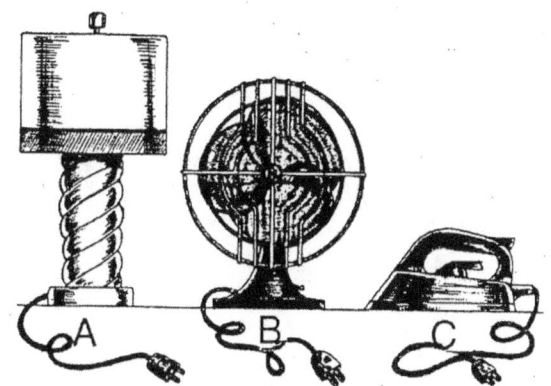

45.

Which uses the most current?

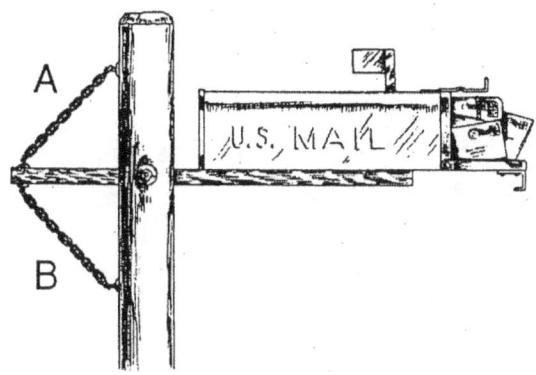

46.

Which one piece of chain will hold up the mailbox shelf?

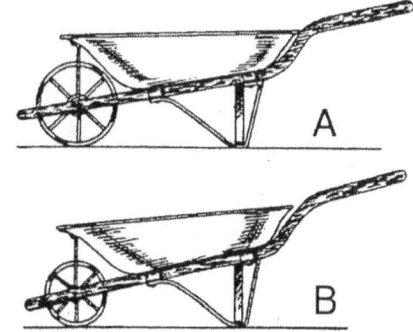

47.

Which wheelbarrow will be easier to roll over uneven ground?

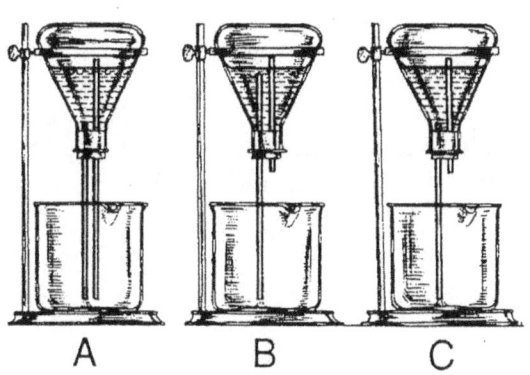

48.

Which jar will let the most water run out?

14 (#1)

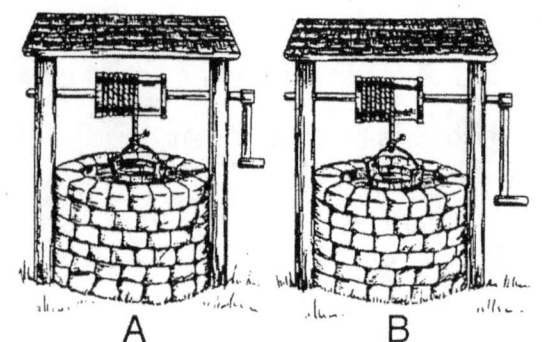

49.

From which well is it easier to raise a bucket of water?

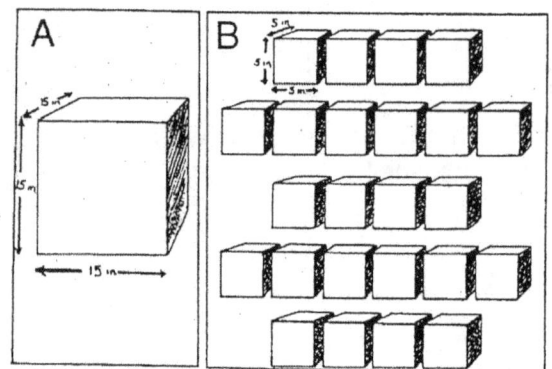

50.

Which weighs more if all these cubes are made of solid iron?

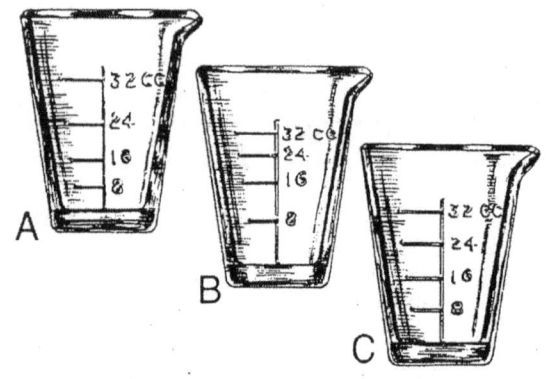

51.

Which measure is properly marked?

52.

Which picture shows the easier way to move the cart over the curb?

15 (#1)

53.

Which plank is more likely to break?

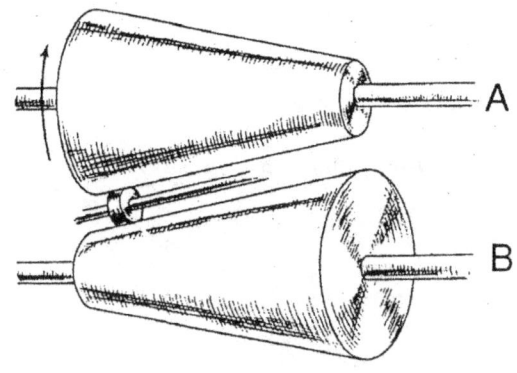

54.

Which shaft will turn faster?

55.

Which weighs more?

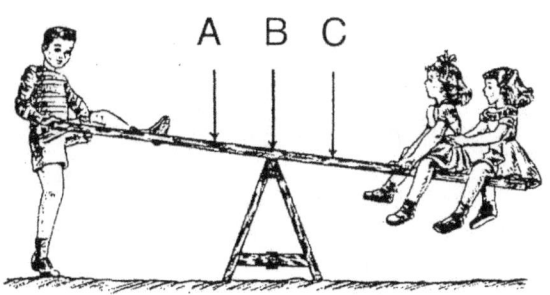

56.

At which point is the seesaw most likely to break?

16 (#1)

57.

Which part of the refrigerator is colder?

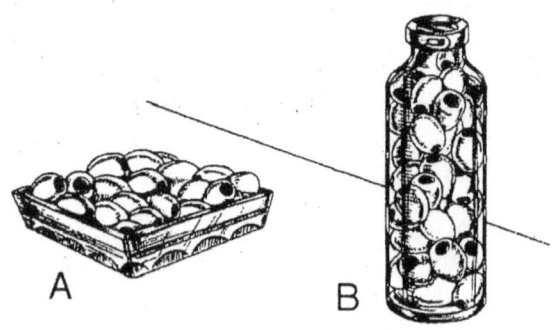

58.

Which olives are larger?

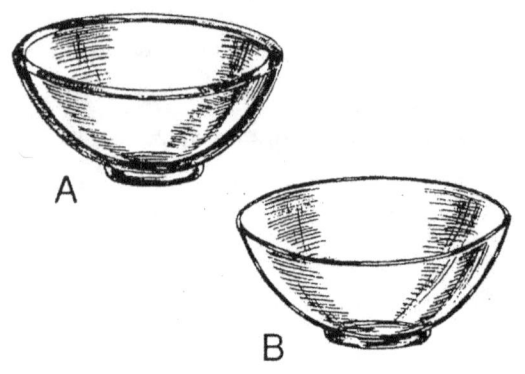

59.

Which bowl will break more easily if put into hot water?

60.

Which will fall faster?

## KEY (CORRECT ANSWERS)

| | | | | | | | |
|---|---|---|---|---|---|---|---|
| 1. | A | 16. | A | 31. | B | 46. | B |
| 2. | B | 17. | B | 32. | B | 47. | B |
| 3. | A | 18. | A | 33. | B | 48. | C |
| 4. | B | 19. | B | 34. | A | 49. | B |
| 5. | A | 20. | A | 35. | B | 50. | B |
| 6. | B | 21. | C | 36. | A | 51. | B |
| 7. | B | 22. | B | 37. | B | 52. | A |
| 8. | B | 23. | B | 38. | A | 53. | B |
| 9. | B | 24. | A | 39. | B | 54. | B |
| 10. | A | 25. | B | 40. | B | 55. | B |
| 11. | A | 26. | A | 41. | A | 56. | A |
| 12. | C | 27. | C | 42. | B | 57. | A |
| 13. | B | 28. | A | 43. | A | 58. | A |
| 14. | A | 29. | A | 44. | A | 59. | B |
| 15. | B | 30. | A | 45. | C | 60. | B |

# MACHINES

## CONTENTS

| | |
|---|---|
| Mechanical Advantage | 1 |
| Calculating Mechanical Advantage | 2 |
| The Lever | 3 |
| Classes of Levers | 3 |
| The Wedge--Inclined Plane | 5 |
| The Pulley | 5 |
| The Wheel and Axle | 6 |

# MACHINES

If you had to open a heavy wooden box but could not pull the boards loose, what would you do? Chances are you would find a bar of some sort and pry the box open. In other words, you would use a *machine*. The bar, or pry, will open the box easily because with it you can exert *more force*. A machine is a device that increases the force that you can exert. Notice that the machine does not supply any more energy. The only energy supply is still your own muscles. But the machine multiplies the force you exert. That is the secret behind every machine, no matter how complicated it may be.

Now, how does the machine multiply force? Basically, the machine trades distance for force. Suppose you need to lift a box two feet. If you know the weight of the box, you can calculate the amount of force needed to lift it. Although the machine cannot supply more energy for lifting, it can exert the same amount of force on the box for a greater distance. That is, instead of lifting the box directly two feet, you pry with a bar, moving the end of the bar ten feet. Thus you have moved five times as far as you would need just to raise the box. But you would need only one-fifth as much force to raise the box. This is the way a machine multiplies force. *It increases the distance a force must move.* The total amount of energy used remains the same.

**Mechanical Advantage**

The amount of increase in force that a machine gives is called its *mechanical advantage*. If a machine will increase the force five times, it has a mechanical advantage of five. If the machine loses force and causes you to work five times as hard, the mechanical advantage is 1/5. Some machines do this. They usually sacrifice force to obtain speed. By using a larger force, the machine can produce faster speeds.

Here's an example of this process: Suppose a box that weighs 1,000 pounds needs to be raised ten feet in the air. The force needed to raise the box is 1,000 poundals. The total amount of energy needed to raise the box is 10,000 foot-poundals. This total energy requirement cannot be changed. But to lift the box straight in the air would take a force of 1,000 poundals, exerted for a distance of ten feet. This is far more than the average man can lift, so a machine must be used.

The machine has a mechanical advantage of ten. Every poundal of force exerted on the machine produces ten poundals of force at the output. Using this machine, one man can raise the box easily. All he must do is exert 100 poundals of force. But the box must be raised ten feet. If the man exerts 100 poundals of force for a distance of ten feet, he will use 1,000 foot-poundals of energy. But that will not raise the box. To raise the box, 10,000 poundals of energy are needed. So the man must exert his 100 poundals of force for 100 feet. Then he will raise the box ten feet into the air.

This principle applies to all machines. The energy used to do work is equal to the force times the distance. If the force is to be increased five times, the distance must be increased five times. For any machine, the *force* times the *distance* the force is exerted must equal the *load* times the distance the load is moved. This can be seen more easily in a formula:

| INPUT | | OUTPUT |
|---|---|---|
| Force x Distance | *must equal* | Load x Distance |

100 lbs x Distance = 1,000 lbs x 10 feet
100 lbs x Distance = 10,000

Distance = $\dfrac{10{,}000}{100} = 100$ feet

You can apply this formula to any machine. The two sides must always balance. Remember that a machine cannot create energy and it cannot destroy energy. It can only multiply the force exerted by multiplying the distance the force is exerted.

You already know many examples of the use of machines. Automobile gears all use this principle. In low gear, the engine turns rapidly and the car moves slowly. The force (engine) moves a long distance while the load (automobile) moves a short distance. This gives an increase in the force shoving the car. That is why low gear is used for a heavy pull.

An example of the reverse process would be an eggbeater. Here, the mechanical advantage is less than one. The force used to turn the beater is increased, but more speed is obtained by doing this. In mechanics, you can never have your cake and eat it too. Force can be increased with a machine, but the force must then be run for a greater distance. If the force is decreased and speed increased, more power is required. The total amount of energy needed to do a job can never be changed.

Remember: Force x Distance *must equal* Load x Distance

## Calculating Mechanical Advantage

How do we find mechanical advantage of a machine? This can be done in two ways. First, compare the amount of force exerted on a machine with the load the machine will lift. If a force of one pound will lift ten pounds, the mechanical advantage of the machine is ten. Second, compare the distance the force moves with the distance the load moves. If the force moves ten feet and the load moves one foot, the mechanical advantage is still ten. The formula (F x D = L x D) will always give the correct answer. We must know either the force and the load, or the distance that both force and load move. Then the mechanical advantage of a machine can be determined.

Of course, this mechanical advantage assumes that the machine is perfect. It also assumes that no energy is lost through friction. In real life this is never true. There is always some loss in a machine. The formula gives the *theoretical* mechanical advantage. To find the *actual* mechanical advantage, we must try the machine and measure. Dividing the actual mechanical advantage by the theoretical mechanical advantage gives the *efficiency* of the machine.

Suppose that a machine has a theoretical mechanical advantage of ten. When the load the machine will lift is actually measured, we find that it is only eight pounds when one pound of force is applied. So the actual mechanical advantage is eight. The machine will do 8/10 of the work that it can theoretically do. Its efficiency is 8/10, or 80 percent.

**The Lever**

A crowbar, a human arm and a steam shovel have one thing in common. They are all levers. The lever is the simplest of all machines. You have used a lever dozens of times. All you need is a rigid bar. Place one end of the bar under the load, run the bar over a fixed point (called the *fulcrum*) and exert force on the other end. A seesaw is a simple lever – the wooden board is the bar, the pipe underneath is the fulcrum. One child is the force; the other child is the load. Children very early learn to adjust the board to make up for a difference in the weight.

Using the force (F), fulcrum (f) and the load on the lever (R, for resistance), we can put the basic principle for all levers into one sentence. The force applied to the lever multiplied by the distance from the force to the fulcrum must always equal the load on the lever multiplied by the distance between the load and the fulcrum. This makes a simple formula: F x D = R x D

As you can see, this is exactly the same as the general formula for all machines. In the figure below, the entire lever is 11 feet long. The fulcrum is one foot from the end, and the force is ten feet from the fulcrum. The resistance, or load, is one foot from the fulcrum. The mechanical advantage of the lever is ten.

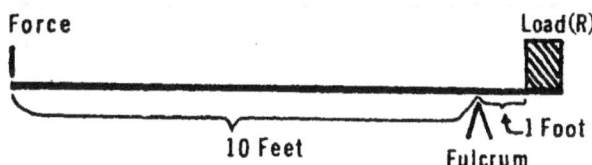

If we place a weight of 100 pounds on this lever, how much force is needed to raise the weight?

F x 10 = 100 x 1
F = 100/10 = 10 poundals

There is also a shortcut. Since the mechanical advantage of the lever is 10, the force will be only 1/10 of the load. Divide the load by 10 and the force is 10 poundals. Now, how far do we have to move the force to raise the load one foot? Again, since the mechanical advantage is 10, this means that the force must move ten times as far as the load. To move the load one foot, the force will have to move ten feet.

**Classes of levers**

Sometimes we cannot place a bar under a load and pry. We may want to place one end of the bar against a wall, and place the load between the force and the fulcrum. Or we may even want to place the load at one end, and apply the force in between. Each of these arrangements is called a *class* of lever. The basic formula applies to all three classes, but they each give a different mechanical advantage.

## FIRST-CLASS LEVER

This is the most common arrangement – like a seesaw. The fulcrum lies *between* the force and the load.

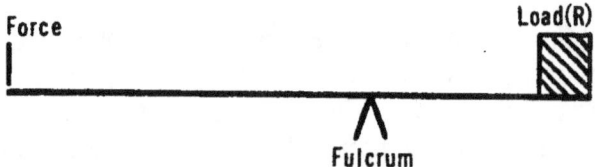

The mechanical advantage of this lever depends upon where the fulcrum is placed. The closer the fulcrum lies to the load (R), the higher the mechanical advantage of the lever.

## SECOND-CLASS LEVER

In the second-class lever, the load lies between the force and the fulcrum. The mechanical advantage of this lever depends upon the placement of the load. The closer the load is to the fulcrum, the higher the mechanical advantage. When the load is close to the force, the mechanical advantage approaches one – no advantage at all.

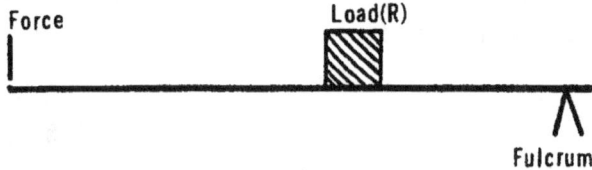

## THIRD-CLASS LEVER

The force is applied between the fulcrum and the load. The mechanical advantage of this lever is always less than one. If the force is applied close to the load, the mechanical advantage is just less than one. It takes more force to raise the load than the load weighs. If the force is applied close to the fulcrum, the mechanical advantage may be small. In fact, it may take 50 times as much force to raise the load as the load weighs. Of course, the loss of mechanical advantage produces a gain in speed. If the mechanical advantage is only 1/100, a movement of one foot by the force produces a movement of 100 feet by the load. The third-class lever cannot be used for heavy loads unless there is a large supply of power available.

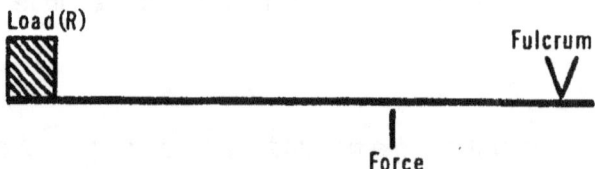

# The Wedge – Inclined Plane

The wedge, the inclined plane and the screw are all based upon the same principle. An inclined plane is just one half of a wedge. All of these machines increase the force exerted by increasing the distance that the force moves. The general formula (Force x Distance = Load x Distance) still applies to these machines. To find the mechanical advantage of the inclined plane or wedge, compare the distance the force moves with the distance the load moves. If a board which is ten feet long is placed against the back of a truck, and the truck bottom is two feet from the ground, the mechanical advantage of the inclined plane is five. This is the theoretical mechanical advantage. In practice, an inclined plane develops a great deal of friction and losses are high. Notice that the load exerts pressure directly toward the ground, and not along the line of the plane. The load distance must always be measured from the ground directly to the top of the lift. The length of the inclined plane is always the distance that the force moves.

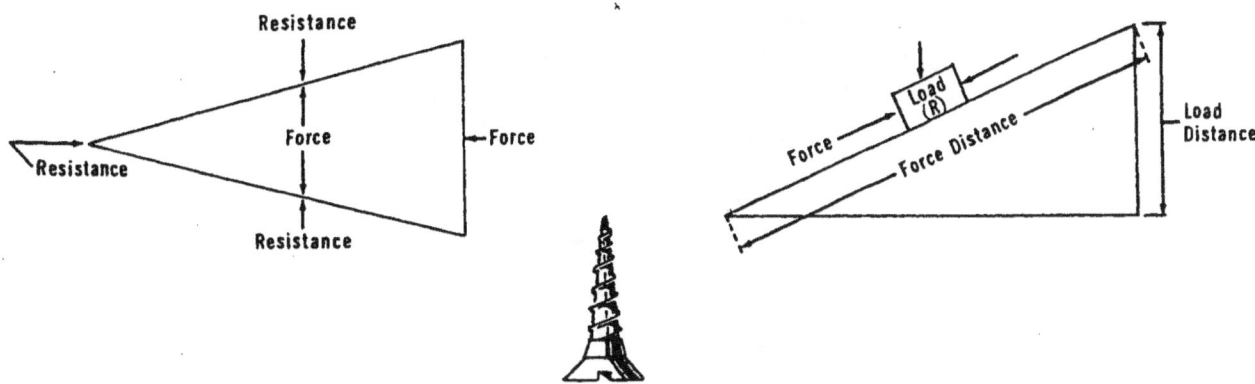

Wedge, Inclined Plane, Screw.

# The Pulley

A pulley is a special form of the lever. The center of the pulley is the fulcrum of the lever. The load is placed on one end of the pulley; the force is exerted at the other end. The pulley shown below (A) has no mechanical advantage, but it is useful because it changes the direction of pull. It is easier to pull down than up. Also shown below (B), the pulley is movable and the rope is fixed on one end. The fulcrum of the lever is now at the left edge of the pulley. The load is in the center, and the force is exerted at the right edge. This is a second-class lever with a mechanical advantage of 2. Of course, the rope will now have to be pulled twice as far as the load is raised.

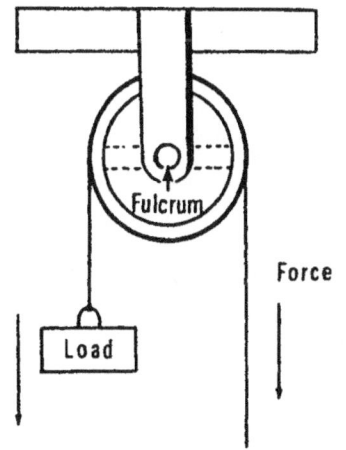

A. Pulley with Mechanical Advantage of One.

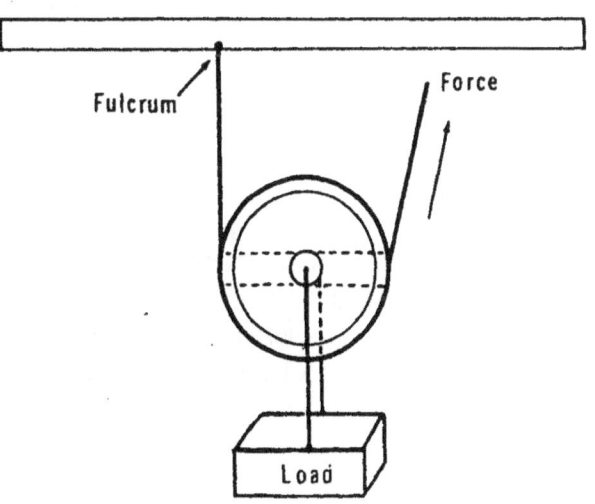

B. Pulley System.

For practical purposes, you can find the mechanical advantage of any pulley system by counting the number of ropes that support the load. Each rope takes an equal share of the load, and the mechanical advantage is equal to the number of supporting ropes. The distance the force must travel can always be found with the general formula for all machines.

**The Wheel and the Axle**

The wheel and axle also form a specialized lever. The figure below is a diagram of a system like the steering wheel of an automobile. One full turn of the large wheel moves 60 inches of distance. One full turn of the small wheel moves six inches. To turn the small rod in the center one inch, the outer wheel must move ten inches. This system has a mechanical advantage of ten. The same general formula applies. The fulcrum of the lever is at the exact center of the wheel. The force is applied at the outer rim of the wheel. The load appears on the small inner ring. This is a second-class lever. The mechanical advantage of the system is the same as the ratio between the distance around the two wheels. You can find the distance around any circle by multiplying the diameter by *pi*.

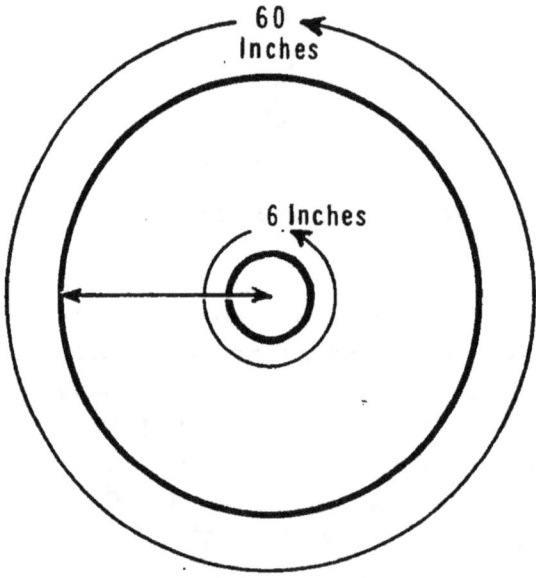

Wheel and Axle.

**Remember...**

- Machines cannot produce energy
- Machines increase force by increasing the distance the force moves
- Theoretical advantage is always more than actual advantage
- Force x Distance always equals Load x Distance

www.ingramcontent.com/pod-product-compliance
Lightning Source LLC
Chambersburg PA
CBHW082212300426
44117CB00016B/2779